The Simple Secrets of

BEING AN ENTREPRENEUR

By Michael S. Melfi
In Conjunction with Rod Hairston

is an attorney who represents emerging companies and established businesses in a wide array of technology and corporate matters. He has extensive experience mentoring, counseling, and securing funding for entrepreneurs, inventors, startups, and small businesses and their disruptive technologies.

Michael was the founder, COO, and general counsel of a multimedia company where he led cutting-edge experiential and digital marketing campaigns for Fortune 500 clients and helped national, industry-leading products and brands monetize and grow their web-based businesses.

Michael's passion is guiding and supporting emerging companies and entrepreneurs. To support these communities, he founded *Be Investable*, an online curriculum for entrepreneurs that provides the tools that help build a successful team, develop strategies for raising capital and produce results.

In addition to writing articles about startups, leadership, and business, Michael has also authored four books aimed to help entrepreneurs gain a better understanding of often seemingly complex areas: *The Simple Secrets of Social Media*, *The Simple Secrets of Intellectual Property*, *The Simple Secrets of Crowdfunding*, and *The Simple Secrets of Being an Entrepreneur*. He can frequently be found touring the country, giving talks and presentations on startups, crowdfunding, and entrepreneurship, as well as interviewing business leaders and entrepreneurs for his weekly podcast, *The Trep Talk*.

Michael is a partner at Bodman PLC, one of the Midwest's leading business law firms that provides counsel to some of the region's most successful companies and individuals on a broad range of issues.

Table of Contents

FOREWARD

You've picked up this book because you are most likely an entrepreneur looking for the inside track to success in what you are doing. If you are reading this you are interested in the guidance, mentoring and tips to help you succeed personally and professionally. In **The Simple Secrets of Being an Entrepreneur**, you'll get all that and more.

Let me tell you a little about myself so you can understand where I get my knowledge and wisdom to write this for you, a fellow entrepreneur who may be struggling and seeking the answer to how to be really successful.

I am a podcast host, speaker, Intellectual Property attorney and an entrepreneur working with and for entrepreneurs for over a decade. I have a vision to empower the entrepreneurial ecosystem through education, collaboration and inspiration. This book is a step towards assisting entrepreneurs on this journey.

I am a self-admitted Serial Entrepreneur – that means I've started and grown multiple businesses. Some have thrived, others didn't, but I have never given up. Some of the successful endeavors you have heard of and others never made it to mainstream, despite their success. Anyway, you did not pick up this book for my autobiography, you could just do a Google search to get that. So, let's focus on what it takes to be successful as an entrepreneur.

That is a personal question, a quest into your inner happiness. I honestly love being an entrepreneur. It gives me great freedom; freedom to take risks, to create my own finish line, to be totally unreasonable with life. Being an entrepreneur allows me to color outside the lines and create clarity where others see chaos. It allows me to stretch beyond what I thought possible. Ultimately, being an entrepreneur has given me an opportunity for self-growth and development - the more that I challenge myself to be better, the more my organization has grown. Finally, being an entrepreneur has required me to make it about others - the customers, the team and my family.

So while some success has financial measurements, much of mine has been defined by other benchmarks.

These may be the same reasons you chose to be an entrepreneur. As I look back, being entrepreneurial started early for me. I first made money with a lawn care business. Your first venture into entrepreneurship could have been with a lemonade stand, taking out the trash, babysitting – think about that first dollar you made; what was it? For me, it was a motivator. Early on I was intrigued by the challenges of business and creating disruptive solutions; as I gained experience, I have grown to love it even more!

My first brush with being a really successful business owner was when I started a pocket sized entertainment and lifestyle magazine, one of the first digital publications, and it became a pioneer in the digital marketing and social media space. I was inspired to start this company by Sir Richard Branson, who got his start in the publishing industry as well.

My background was in traditional print publishing and I saw that there was hesitancy in transitioning to digital media. Publishing companies wanted to wait to 'see how it goes,' but I knew that it was the future of the industry. How could it not be with everyone looking 'online' for information, it would only be a matter of time before they looked online for their enjoyment too.

So I took the leap and launched one of the first digital magazines ever. Stepping into the abyss wasn't always easy – I had to be fearless and bold. I visited most major brands and their agencies in New York, Miami and Chicago that generally would only advertise in print, and convinced them that a presence online with my publication was the way to go. They were hesitant and I was insistent that the future was online and if they wanted to capture the young audience, who would become the new mainstream, they needed to jump on my bandwagon.

Here I was a relatively young person telling these well-established, experienced executives to take a leap of faith in my magazine and team. I often approached the meetings seeking to understand what their needs were and developed experiential marketing solutions for them.

That often included answering questions regarding KPIs and other return on advertising measures. I showed them the statistics of Facebook, the power of Twitter and influenced them to understand that these were just the tip of the iceberg. With the use of social media we could tap into the target audience like never before.

It was hard work, it was daunting at first and yes, fearful, but with an unflinching belief in what I saw as the future of publishing and a great opportunity, I overcame many obstacles and personal deceptions.

I was right; people were hungry for that familiar feel only online and easily accessible on their laptops and other mobile devices. Today it's so commonplace we don't think about not using our laptops, tablets or phones to access information and entertainment. For me, it all started with utilizing the Internet and various social media platforms to develop an online presence for my company that resulted in it ranking in the top 1% of all websites globally. I believe our success with the magazine was partly due to the belief that you have to <u>be disruptive with innovation</u> – don't be afraid to take risks and push the envelope, no matter what field you are in!

There are always going to be roadblocks - and there were plenty, but what company doesn't face them? Attitude is everything – you need to look at the glass as half full and look for solutions at each roadblock. Then execute on those solutions – that's where success comes from. Once I decided to focus and get through the obstacles, they disappeared from my mind and I knew how to avoid them next time. I know the key was a strong belief in my business idea and on the ability to execute.

Based on my own experience, I began to mentor and consult with other entrepreneurs, startups, and small to medium businesses. Over the last decade I have assisted hundreds of small business owners and entrepreneurs in their life either personally or professionally. Most recently with the advent of modern day Crowdfunding, I have had the opportunity of being actively involved in the industry as an author, speaker and consultant. This experience was very eye opening for me, which we will talk about in detail in this book, as there was the conversation that transitioned my thinking thanks to Mr. Rod Hairston. The Models used and references in this book are based on Rod Hairston's book **Are You Up For The Challenge?**

During this time and through my personal experiences, I noticed patterns in the behaviors that are common to an entrepreneur. I began to notice obstacles and issues that repeatedly faced entrepreneurs. Personally, I faced many of these obstacles and overcame them, and the people I was working with, at times, did not seem to be able to overcome the same obstacles. They became fearful and failed to take risks. Through this journey, I realized it wasn't the tactical side of being an entrepreneur they were uneducated in; it was the mental side.

When I say mental side, I mean they didn't have the right habits, focus, attitude and beliefs they needed to truly succeed beyond a certain point. Oh yes, many of them did succeed, but they suffered through unnecessarily instead of enjoying the journey; they were frightened and fearful, their belief in their idea, business or service waned. They were scattered and unfocused. All of which are roadblocks they didn't really know how to overcome. While they may have achieved certain status or significance, they had not achieved success or the ultimate goals for why they became an entrepreneur in the first place.

For example, from a tactical standpoint, they could buy a book on writing a business plan, but if they stumbled with getting started, they would quit and ignore the fact that they needed a plan of action. Not knowing where they were headed, not having the strategy in place and the steps to get to their ultimate vision was a huge obstacle. For some, maybe they focused and started on the business plan only to get stalled at one element, such as the marketing plan they wanted to include in their plan. Because of that one element, that lack of confidence in that one area, that business plan never got written – they didn't know how to overcome their uncertainty surrounding that portion of the plan. And yet others would attend all the meetings, buy all the programs, hire all the consultants and coaches, yet they could never reach the ultimate performer status they yearned for. So, what was holding them back? What was the missing link?

This is what drove me to write this book - I have watched time and again the same types of mistakes being made by entrepreneurs at all stages of their growth – not just the Angel funding or startup phase, but successful 30-year entrepreneurs who still struggled with basic obstacles. After seeing the repetitive patterns creating setbacks and many times, failure, I was driven to write this book in an effort to empower entrepreneurs.

After all of our research and studies we found that successful entrepreneurs, with their teams, excel in certain areas. We further identified the characteristics that make for success.

My goal with this book is to address the entrepreneur's thinking patterns, working habits, attitude and focus – all key to success in Business Strategy, Business Development and Business Knowledge.

If you are a serious entrepreneur, faced with obstacles and uncertainty, this book is for you. Even if you are contemplating starting a company or trying to get an idea funded, this book will help you get focused and develop the mindset and behaviors required to succeed.

The case studies in this book are based on the seven levels of deception from the Cycle of Growth Model based off the Models by Rod Hairston in his book **Are You Up For The Challenge?** These are our best, real-world examples of actual entrepreneurs that we've dealt with that exemplify the levels of deception.

The good news is that some were able to recognize their deception, that the issue was them and not anyone or anything else, and they changed. They worked hard to change and used the tools we've discussed in this book; habits, focus, attitude, and self talk. They worked to excel at the characteristics we've outlined, and transformed into the Identity of an Entrepreneur.

See if any of these case studies remind you of anyone - including yourself!

WHY ENTREPRENEURS FAIL

- **90% of entrepreneurs fail in the first 5 years?**

- **And 9 out of every 10 borrowers get rejected for a loan from a traditional lending source?**

- **Or that 99% of entrepreneurs and early stage companies do not receive their funding from Angel Investors and Venture Capitalists (VCs)?**

Not great statistics are they? I get asked repeatedly, 'why does this happen, why do entrepreneurs fail?' It's really pretty easy to figure out.

Resources could be time, money, energy, as well as tools, software, expertise. For every industry the list of resources is different, but is still correlated to the entrepreneur's success.

By the time many Entrepreneurs seek out assistance for help and guidance, many times they have already exhausted all of their resources. They are looking for a secret to success, or a magic pill, a knight in shining armor to save them from their situation. The fact of the matter is that it is usually in these moments

when an entrepreneur shines through or is created. Martin Luther King Jr. once said "the ultimate measure of a man is not where he stands in moments of comfort and convenience, but where he stands at times of challenge and controversy."

It is in these moments where we as humans chose to react - do we hold fast to our beliefs and move through the obstacle transforming us into the success we had envisioned, or do we choose to fall down and not get back up?

- it is ok to fall down and that is going to happen a lot, however getting back up and persisting through the obstacles is where transformation to success occurs.

These "times of challenge and controversy" are what we call 'Deception', which we will cover in detail in later chapters, but ultimately goes back to why entrepreneurs fail. It's a question we've been exploring and have sought to cure, or at least address in this book and transform through education, collaboration and inspiration in our programs and content.

It is painful to realize that failure continues to plague the entrepreneurial eco-system despite all the available resources, despite all of the strategy and tactics that exist to help. Despite a plethora of money sources, investors looking for deals with intelligent, talented and creative team members, entrepreneurs still are not reaching their ultimate success.

It is common for an entrepreneur to wake up in the morning wanting more, wanting to succeed and seeing the vision of where they want to go, where they want to take an idea and company. Maybe they've already bought the car of their dreams and now they're figuring out how to pay for it; maybe they've already built the business plan, the blueprint has been created for they to follow to get to their dream. Maybe they've begun to hire the right people, or maybe they're still struggling with how to get there. Despite this progress, there will still be obstacles; there will still be situations they must face to get to where they want to go on the journey.

The Identity of a Successful Entrepreneur comes from simply achieving your goal of achieving it, to be happy.

This remained on my quote board for almost a year until one day I finally got it. Happiness is a way of being and achieving success is a way of being as well. So, as entrepreneurs, we can be happy and achieving success at each moment of the journey. So success comes from having the Identity of an Entrepreneur. Success is in the ability to overcome failure starting with the proper beliefs and the right ideals. It all begins with the individual's ability to go inward to develop their intra and interpersonal skills to become stronger, to be able to come out the other side of the journey having mastered how to overcome adversity. And the great part is that WE get to define success for ourselves. Many people think it is measured by how rich an individual is, however the true definition is in how happy an individual is.

Dissecting the entrepreneurial journey reveals a few key areas that are critical to success: the mindset, the behaviors, the habits and ultimately the focus an entrepreneur has on their idea, their service, and their business – their journey. We will be discussing these areas in more detail in upcoming chapters.

At the end of the day, an entrepreneur's resources will run out long before their desire or their will to succeed. The magic pill, the knight in shining armor, the secret to be a successful entrepreneur is the ability to move through these obstacles, to move through deception, and that requires focus.

When they first start out, most of the focus will be on their product, the prototype, the service and building up awareness on a small, manageable scale. But as a business grows, they will need to expand the focus to other areas. Whether starting out or growing, they still will need to have the Identity of a Successful Entrepreneur.

Another area that is very important is to have the right habits. It's so easy to focus on putting out fires. In that mindset they are unable to stay on course toward what needs to get done, but rather they are reacting to whatever is happening at that time. When there are strong habits, they will overpower and win in the distracted phases and the obstacles an entrepreneur faces.

Habits are built up over time and can be challenging to master in the beginning,

but they will, over time, become automatic. By building the habits that help to focus on business goals, they are telling the unconscious mind that this is the way they want to be moving forward, this is the way they want to run their business, this is the way they want to work to be successful. Since habits live in the unconscious mind, they will start to see productive habits take hold and produce the results desired.

You may think you already have these habits in place, but do you? If you are the go-to person who puts out every fire, before a day ends you may look back and feel like you've accomplished a great deal, but did your actions really move you toward the goals and outcomes you want for your company? Probably not.

To start focused habits, you could start as small as committing to call three sales leads per day for your Business Development, reviewing media about your competitors for your Business Knowledge. It could be blocking out a specific time of day to focus on those calls, and use that time to mine for new business, to work on your marketing, sales, hiring, vendor relations, research, etc. If you scheduled out time for each of these types of tasks that will lead to accomplishing your goal, and actually focus during that time, you will develop a habit of making three calls a day, keeping up with your competition and industry, mining for new business, etc. One action that moves you toward your goal, consistently executed, will become a habit. It will begin to feel a normal part of your day, especially when you start to see the results.

Going back to the beginning of this chapter, Entrepreneurs fail because they learn too late that they don't have the right the mindset, the behaviors, the habits and ultimately the focus needed to succeed before their resources run out or can be replenished.

Working with the VICTIM ENTREPRENEUR

Case Study: *Not my fault!*

When you hear 'victim' what comes to mind? Ever met someone who blames others and circumstances for where they are at in life? In the Entrepreneurial eco system, the victims look outside of themselves when things don't go right and that can lead to deep discomfort.

If you're not sure what I mean, let me tell you about my experience with the Victim Entrepreneur. I had the opportunity to work with several professionals in the Health & Wellness Industry. They had amazing knowledge of their industry, what the past held, what the trends were, and both of these professionals could anticipate trends and changes in their industry. They were very creative and could create compelling strategies that could lead their companies to growth. In my experience, their strategies were on target and would help any business to succeed in growing.

So why do I look upon them as the "Victim"? They could come up with the best strategies I'd ever seen; they understood the big picture and how their business could fit into it, their strategies were sound and it was exciting to see that they understood that part of the business.

However, when it came to execution, they fell apart. They would come up with excuses as to why something didn't work and usually they blamed others or the circumstances rather than take responsibility for the problems, instead of looking inward. You may have worked with people like this; you'll hear that it wasn't them their fault, it was the software, the phones, vendor X and manufacturer Y that were at fault. Instead of owning situations and accepting any thing responsibility, they play the blame game.

Looking closer at the situation, perhaps it was their fault. Perhaps they didn't purchase the recommended software upgrade, perhaps the phones were faulty before they started, or the vendor and manufacturer followed the specs they were given, only to find out the specs were wrong.

Blaming outside forces and becoming the victim of circumstances is a habit formed somewhere in their life. Rather than accept responsibility when things went wrong, which would be very uncomfortable, they blamed others or circumstances beyond their control.

Some of these professionals were very successful, but when things didn't go well, it was always someone else's fault.

Fortunately, one of these professionals finally realized that they were the problem and worked to transform from the Identity of a Victim into the Identity of an Entrepreneur. They stopped blaming others, looked to themselves as the issue and learned from their mistakes. They welcomed that uncomfortable feeling as a sign that they were about to transform. They started to take the recommendations of experts, connected and went over specs with vendors more closely and improved overall communication. They started to complement others instead of always finding fault. And the biggest change – they were happier.

If you are reading this and believe I am wrong, this is a red flag for you to look at yourself and your recent actions.

Lesson: *Any entrepreneur can change their situation. Looking for answers within should be the first step taken when things become difficult or don't go as planned.*

CREATING FOCUS IN THE LIFE OF AN ENTREPRENEUR

If you are anything like me, as an entrepreneur it's really easy to get distracted, really easy to get off course, it's really easy to start finding a million and one fires I need to work on, and not focus on the one thing that will lead to success.

What distractions come between you and your one thing?

If you're working from home, undone household chores staring at you, or a pet, or children needing your attention can pull you away from what you are working on. Working distractions like unexpected phone calls, constantly checking emails and fires you are expected to put out also take focus away from the one thing that can lead to success that hour, day, week or quarter.

Other things show up as interrupts such as procrastination, inconsistency, an impatience to work on things immediately instead of waiting for a better time. Sometimes it's new ideas that keep popping into your head that divert your attention. You want to start on every one of them right as you get them!

These can all be good things, and important in the right circumstances. You can't ignore the crying child or the dog scratching at the back door; you can't ignore your key customer that calls with an emergency. Things happen that are important but how do you overcome these distractions and really get focused on what's important to build and grow your business? Through your focus.

There are   developed by Rod Hairston that are important to entrepreneurs. They are:

1. *WHAT YOU FOCUS ON YOU FIND*
2. *WHAT YOU FOCUS ON SEEMS REAL*
3. *WHAT YOU FOCUS ON WILL GROW*
4. *WHAT YOU FOCUS ON YOU BECOME*

I had a situation myself where a business deal went sour. I had a good month that I spent on that bad deal. My mentor challenged me and asked 'how much time do you waste not being focused on your next deal, on what needs to be done, on your next client?'

When I added it up and it was hundreds of hours. He was right I was wasting precious time. Immediately, when I was able to stop focusing on that bad deal, I created ten or fifteen hours a day of time to focus on the things that made me money, that grew my business, that supported my culture – all the things that as entrepreneurs we want. It even gave me time to work out, time to go to a yoga class – all the things that meant a lot to me personally. I took myself to dinner.

All those things all of a sudden became possible as an entrepreneur because I didn't have to spend my time focusing on something that was actually really negative in and of itself, but also just distracting me from being productive.

That's what we're going to look at next.

Just like in my situation, when I was able to clear out some of the obstacles I had, the Deception I had, I had a lot of free time to then start to focus on other things, important things to me.

You may have the preconceived notion of what Focus means to each of us –

success, more tools, better results. Ultimately achieving what you really want out of your business as an Entrepreneur if you have focus.

The definition of **Focus**:

- *THE STATE OR QUALITY OF HAVING OR PRODUCING CLEAR VISUAL DEFINITION.*
- *THE CENTER OF INTEREST OR ACTIVITY.*
- *PAY PARTICULAR ATTENTION TO.*

Focus is really being able to hone in – you've heard the phrase 'laser focused' and that is what we're talking about.

Focusing attention means aiming your mental energy in a specific direction rather than giving equal consideration to anything and everything that comes to mind. The term multitasking is really this lack of focus on one specific thing. Being focused to the extent that there are no distractions that can penetrate that focus, is our definition.

As an entrepreneur, how often do you sit at your desk and there are ten things you need to do; check your email, Facebook, send this person a text, write everything down, and by the way did I feed the dog, did I take care of my bills? And all of a sudden you have seventy things going on in your life and you're not focused at all!

Have you ever been in a conversation when someone was talking to you and looking right at you and they ask you a questions and you say, 'What did you say?' Have you ever been in a business meeting and the person talking starts to sound like a character in a Charlie Brown special 'Wha Wha Wha?'

Have you ever been in a business meeting trying to make a sale or in an interview trying to hire someone and all of a sudden you tune them out completely? These are examples of being distracted, the lack of focus, that's what we're talking about here. How do you not lose that?

Let's do a quick exercise around Focus. Get comfortable in your seat, put a timer on for 30 seconds. Then close your eyes and start to visualize and think to yourself, 'What is the vision for my business?' It could be what your business looks like, how much money you'll have, it could be how many employees you'll have, it could be the kind of car you drive. Are you able to keep focused on what your vision is? What does your free time look like, what does your weekend look like, what do your evenings look like?

Did you lose track of what you were thinking about?

Did you hold the vision in your mind, or were you thinking about something else?

How detailed, specifically, did you get?

That's an example of focus. Let's try another exercise!

This time, get comfortable in your seat, put a timer on for 30 seconds, close your eyes and think about nothing – blankness. Just relax and let your mind be quiet.

Did you think 'is 30 seconds up yet'?

Did you let your mind go blank and focus on nothing?

If so, that's the ability to train your mind.

As entrepreneurs we spend a lot of time thinking. We have a million and one ideas. How do we stop that and just pause and get clear on just the one thing you need to do in that moment.

For some people, it is easy to focus on nothing, for others it's almost impossible. Sometimes when the mind is clear, clarity of what to do next comes to you. Use these exercises when you need some help in focusing. Get clarity around your vision, and clear your mind of the 'tasks' you need to get done and relax, recharge, then refocus on the one thing you really need to turn your attention to.

When we work with entrepreneurs, Focus is one of the models we use; the ability to work on what we call the 'mental gym.' When you go to a gym to work out – you run, work your physical muscles, maybe ride a bike. When you do a good workout you end up being tired and sore. It's because you worked your muscles. The other side of a workout is that you had the opportunity to grow as a person.

Your mind works the same way. We call it the 'mental gym'; being able to do something and go back and do it again becoming consistent and proficient. As entrepreneurs we are going to have distractions, and they can be frustrating. There are going to be obstacles to overcome, hurdles you will have to deal with, and as you get stronger and better at overcoming these roadblocks, you will be able to be an entrepreneur and be as relaxed as you were when you did the mind clearing exercise.

The Four Laws of Focus can be used no matter what your business and the distractions you need to overcome. The ability to refocus by taking a moment to clear your mind when distractions come into play, is critical for your success.

The Four Laws Of Focus:

1. ***WHAT YOU FOCUS ON YOU FIND***
2. ***WHAT YOU FOCUS ON SEEMS REAL***
3. ***WHAT YOU FOCUS ON WILL GROW***
4. ***WHAT YOU FOCUS ON YOU BECOME***

If you focus on something, your energy will find it. We've all experienced this

Law of Focus. Have you ever been looking for something and suddenly found it? You focused on finding the object and lo and behold, you found it!

Another example is when you've looked for a new car. Once you buy it you suddenly notice how many people are driving the same car! You never noticed before because you weren't focused on it. How many times have you said, 'I really need X' and suddenly you are bombarded with people with that skill set or expertise?

What you focus on is critical to your success. If you focus on the sour deal like I did, you may find more sour deals! If you focus on failure, even in your inner self talk, that's what you'll find.

If you focus on success, on building a great team, on the best location for your business, guess what? You will find it!

That's the first law of focus; what you focus on you find.

The second law of focus is about what you thought of becoming real...feels real. For example, you go to a spooky movie, and afterwards every dark room, every sound seems that much more creepy to you. What you focus on will seem real. Another example is when someone says something like 'it's hot in here' and before they said that you hadn't noticed the temperature. All of a sudden you start to think about it being hot and then you notice that, yes, you are hot!

So someone, an entrepreneur, who says they don't think there's much business in this city at all, well, you don't want to hang out with them at all. You get too many of this type of person in a room and it starts to become perpetual. It will seem to be the truth, and for those people it is the truth. Since what you focus on becomes real, ask yourself, 'is this the reality I want?' Negative people will pull you in a negative direction and that is what you will focus on; negative people can influence your focus.

Put one procrastinator in a room and they admit they have trouble getting things done and the next person will agree and say they have a hard time getting things done. And on it goes. And while it is true that it *is* hard to get things done, the more and more we focus on the difficulty, the more that difficulty becomes real.

The quicker we change our attitude to 'I'm getting it done', the quicker you break the cycle. Break the negative self-talk today, and tomorrow and the day after that and you will see how quickly procrastination is not your issue. You will find yourself focusing on other, more important issues.

What you focus on seems real. Our minds are so strong that our conscious and subconscious are what's real to us. It's where everything lies. If you let that control and dictate where you are going, you will be out of control.

Remember when you were a child and a parent or grandparent would tell you a bedtime story, maybe about their life as a child? You believed it was real didn't you? It seemed real to you until they told you it wasn't true. It seemed real because that's all you ever knew from their stories.

That happens with your mind, the more you hear something and the more you believe it, it just seems real. If you put ceilings around what's possible or what you can do, you become stifled and limited. It's important as an entrepreneur that you don't let that happen.

You avoid that by constantly focusing on your vision, how wonderful it is. Focus on it until it *feels* real. Let that feeling permeate everything that you do and see how quickly you notice the negative and break the cycle.

What You Focus On Will Grow

The more energy you direct towards something the bigger it will become (both good and bad). Have you ever had a really good client and took actions around that client, keep focusing on them? For me, what I found is that client's business grew into a larger, better client.

Have you ever had an employee that was great and kept getting better the more you told them they were wonderful? On the other side, have you had a team member that is a challenge or difficult? As a manager, that happens. As the employee, you may notice that after you had a bad review it kept going downhill from there? It's because the focus, positive or negative, made the situation grow.

We've seen movements created by people, we've seen videos go viral - this happened because people focused on that movement or that one video. Stop and think about this; it's a video. There are millions of videos on the Internet, but when we, as a society, start to focus on it, on just one video, the next thing you know the person is on The Ellen DeGeneres Show!

What made it so funny? A bunch of us focused on it and made it go viral, that's all it is. Your business is the same; it's the exact same thing.

What you focus on will grow. Even a solo-preneur will see this in action; what that sole person focuses on, will grow. The minute they get another person in their organization and the two of them start to focus, it will turn into three, once the three start to focus it will turn into six and go from there! That's where culture is born, how people build strong cultures within their business, because they start focusing on it.

Culture is more than a nice office, more than games that the staff can play, it is a mindset that comes from the leadership and trickles down to the team. A collaborative, creative, open and empowering culture starts with the first employee you hire. If you are driven and demanding, your culture may turn into one that gets results, but through stress instead of excitement. Developing your culture is very important as you grow so you maintain the empowerment of your staff, foster creativity and innovation to grow even more.

When you start to focus on the core competencies in your business, that's what will grow. That's what's worth putting your energy into; that's what ultimately becomes bigger.

The fourth law of Focus, What you Focus On You Become, you've most likely seen throughout your life and maybe didn't realize it. Do you think the valedictorian of the class ever focused on anything else? Remember that person in your class? Did you ever wonder what they did all day to become valedictorian?

They focused on it to the exclusion of almost anything else. It is ALL they cared about. There was no question in their mind that they were going to become the valedictorian, and nothing would deter them from that road.

There are many examples of entrepreneurs that managed to focus and were determined. One prime example is Steve Jobs who was kicked out of his own company before age thirty when everyone told him he was crazy for trying to make a dent in the Universe.

They didn't think Albert Einstein was going to get through high school. Oprah Winfrey was told she wasn't good enough to be on television and was told to think about doing something else.

If these people had listened and focused on what others told them, where would they be now? If you look at someone who is successful, they have defined what is important to them and that is their idea of success. It's not always money, it could be where they live, a great family, driving the car they want, having a great business, maybe it's giving back to the world, doing something with their church or other organization – the people doing it – they are focused on it and are not doing anything else! They know nothing else but doing that and that's what they become.

They didn't wake up a star in their field, it took focus. As you continue to focus on your goals you will become what you focus on. I knew a boy who was a terrible reader and he focused very hard on becoming a reader; today he's an author. It took focus and determination to become what he focused on.

This is the key to visualization, like we did in the mind exercises. Without the visualization around your business knowledge, strategy, development and mindset, you have nothing to work for; no vision or goal. In the exercise you had 30 seconds to visualize your business. What if you could do that everyday when you get going? What if everyday you started out like that and started your day with that vision? What would your attitude be? What would your focus be? If you could pick just one of your ideas and stick with it for just one week, where would it be at the end of that week?

Have you ever met someone that told you they were going to do or be something specific, like a fireman, a nurse, a doctor, and they actually became that? That's a mindset and that's focus.

Working with professional athletes, we found that most of them from the time they were little kids visualized themselves becoming what they ended up becoming. They saw themselves winning the Little League World Series and then the next goal and then going to play in the pro's. They saw it ever since they were small. It was all they focused on and they became what they focused on.

The Four Laws Of Focus:

1. **WHAT YOU FOCUS ON YOU FIND**
2. **WHAT YOU FOCUS ON SEEMS REAL**
3. **WHAT YOU FOCUS ON WILL GROW**
4. **WHAT YOU FOCUS ON YOU BECOME**

The 4 laws of focus may sound the same but they all have a little difference variance on focus. When you put them all together they are compelling and what you'll find is that you will be more successful in your personal life and your professional life when you follow these laws.

Do you focus on one or more of these critical areas?

- *MARKETING STRATEGY*
- *SALES*
- *BUSINESS DEVELOPMENT*
- *RESEARCH & DEVELOPMENT*
- *FUNDRAISING*
- *ACQUIRING TALENT*
- *MANAGING DAILY OPERATIONS*

Successful businesses focus on ALL of these everyday. If the leader is not focusing on one, they have a team member whose role it is to focus on that area. As a startup business without employees, the leader should focus on each of these areas every day.

If you aren't marketing, you aren't going to generate new clients and you aren't going to make sales. Without sales you aren't going to pay the bills. Without business development you aren't going to continue to grow your business, find new people, new partnerships, or new opportunities. Without Research and Development you won't be able to improve your product or services, you aren't going to be able to grow your team. Without Fundraising you aren't going to have the funding in place, necessarily, to run your business. If you are doing a great job with sales, then maybe you don't need fundraising yet. Are you acquiring talent, building a team, building a culture, or finding a co-founder? Are you day-to-day being able to manage the operations of your business?

Or are you not able to focus but rather let procrastination get in the way? Your dog's barking gets in the way, deciding to go for a workout in the middle of the day gets in the way. Something else gets in the way and you are not focused on these critical aspects of your business. And maybe you aren't letting something else "get in the way" but rather avoiding the tasks that are a little uncomfortable for you.

You won't get there overnight, but look at each of these as a pound weight. You couldn't lift all of them your first day at the gym, but if you go back and practice on a regular basis and stay focused, you can easily lift five or ten pounds.

If there is anything on the list you don't want to deal with, the more we focus on not dealing with that category, the more it will become a problem. The quicker you admit you don't want to deal with it, that you want to do something else, like invent, or create, you better find some talent to help you. You should still have a working knowledge of each area; you cannot sell your invention if you don't have some way to do marketing, sales and development.

When we talk about focusing, it's being able to focus and putting together a team that can focus on all these areas in your business to create the success you want. If you had your business firing on all these areas, you'd be operating pretty well!

That's what focus is about. It's a mental state where you are able to visualize, to hold that vision and the ability to stay there; and it's the ability to see what that outcome is, the end result you're really going for. When you lose focus on what your end goal is, you get distracted.

Another analogy on focus is a high school runner I knew. Once when cheering him on, his Dad said 'he's not going to do well today.' He was a lap ahead of everyone else on the track, but his father said he wouldn't set a personal record that day, which was his goal. When asked why he thought that, he pointed to his son. "He's not focused. Watch his head. He's looking around, he's paying attention to everything but what he needs to do in front of him, which is take the next step."

Here's someone who was a lap ahead of everyone else, but whose goal was to set a personal record and ultimately to get a scholarship and go on to college, and he was busy running looking at the birds. Even though he was better than everyone else, he was successful; he still wasn't focused on what he really wanted, a personal record.

It's easy to be complacent and lose focus when you're out in front of the pack. Focus isn't just for when you are struggling or procrastinating, it could be for the top salesperson or the top entrepreneur. If you don't stay focused on what that ultimate goal is, that 'why' for being there, you will get distracted and bad habits will set in.

Focus is about putting one step in front of the other and making sure you stay focused on what's next.

Working with the THE RUT DWELLER ENTREPRENEUR

Case Study: *This is too Hard!*

None of us likes to feel uncertainty and discomfort and feel as if we don't know what we're doing, or feel like a failure at what we're trying to do. I know personally I don't like it! When we stick to just what we know, we cut off opportunity, we remove the possibility and a business has little room to grow.

Working with many technology and Internet-based businesses, I ran into many entrepreneurs that were 'Rut Dwellers'. They had a very strong skill set or expertise within their industry and often had a wonderful idea for a new technology or Internet-based business. Many times they had managed to secure funding – every entrepreneur's dream. Their investors believed in the business and put their money behind it, believing they would get a return on the investment when the business performed well.

Many of these businesses launch with attention from national publications. The reviews were extremely positive. However, the anticipated influx of customers was disappointing and it performed below expectation – it just didn't work like they wanted and wasn't getting the traction it needed. The app got some downloads then lost customer interest. The website had a lot of functionality and amazing features but loaded slowly and had bad customer experience and lost traffic. The team spent all the money on development and technology and lacked the resources for business development and the growth hacking to be successful.

When things started to get a little too hard and overwhelming, the partners started to become unavailable for meetings, wouldn't invest the effort needed to turn it around. When the funding ran out they simply quit. They didn't like the situation because it felt very uncomfortable. They would rather not deal with it at all then be a part of the solution.

They remained stagnant in their efforts to make the business work. They didn't try to push through because it was too uncomfortable. They'd rather stay in what they knew, their rut, instead of finding solutions. As entrepreneurs, we know to pivot, to spin, and to brainstorm on how to make it work; that's what entrepreneurs do. Many times this is called a 'pivot.'

Of course, a Rut Dweller Entrepreneur can be successful - if they stay out of the rut. The partners in the Internet-based venture were all successful in their respective industries. Yet, in this case, the partners simply quit when they hit obstacles, they shrugged and held up their hands in surrender. They didn't want to accept that the concept was good, but it had problems and it just needed some work. They didn't like how it felt to struggle, to have it not work.

This was a new industry for each of them and demonstrates the importance of business knowledge and business strategy is for every industry and business. If they had the business knowledge needed for the new industry, they would have had the strategies in place to anticipate and address some of the pitfalls. They would have understood how to pivot, to change and to adjust. But instead they stayed in the more familiar rut, where it was more comfortable, less overwhelming. Instead they it resulted in an unsuccessful business instead of a thriving business.

The key is to pivot, to adapt to market and customers quickly as opposed to getting stuck in the rut. Optimal performance comes from reducing the obstacles, issues, ruts and mistakes quicker than resources run out.

They did not understand that the entrepreneurial journey has ups and downs, especially in that online industry. This is an example of a business that would have thrived if they had taken the time to understand the business, gained the business knowledge and had strategies in place for the situations that arose.

Lesson: *Realize life is dynamic; things can never stay the same – especially for entrepreneurs. It's critical that an entrepreneur have business knowledge and business strategy so they know what they are doing and understand when and how to pivot. Your industry is constantly changing, growing or shrinking – you make the choice – stay in the rut of comfort and stagnation, or change with it.*

THE IDENTITY MODEL

Did you know that Identity is the strongest force in human nature? Staying consistent with your Identity, the one you have for yourself, is the strongest force you will ever have. Our habits, our beliefs and our values, at an unconscious level create our Identity. Thus, identity is so important to understand as we go through the journey of an Entrepreneur.

By understanding Identity and how that Identity is created and grown we can develop as individuals, we can learn, we can continue to transform into ultimately what we are looking to become. In the case of an entrepreneur, it is the Identity of a successful Entrepreneur.

The Identity Model is outlined in more detail in Rod Hairston's book, **Are You Up For The Challenge?** We've taken the model and explain it in this chapter and in the next chapter as we apply it directly to being an entrepreneur.

There are three ways of shaping and creating your Identity.

The first is a significant emotional event, the second is through conditioning and the third is by your environment. They are all are important and can happen in our lives in different ways.

Just like it sounds, this method of creating change is a significant event that has a lot of emotion around it. For example, let's look at Michael Jordan getting cut from his Junior High basketball team. At some core level that event pushed him

-- it propelled him. His habits, his beliefs his values changed at an unconscious level to become one of, if not the greatest, basketball players of all times.

Personally, as a young adult I had a very significant car accident. It was a significant emotional event for me. It changed my habits, it changed my values and it changed my beliefs, transforming my life, in a very positive way.

We've all had different emotional events. Some of them are great and some of them are not. People have had good and bad relationships. We've all lost individuals in our lives, and loved ones. In some cases, we've experienced terrible situations, where we may have been picked on, bullied, even abused. Failures in business or school, or huge disappointments are emotional events too. Maybe that acceptance letter from the school of your dreams turned out to be a rejection letter. Perhaps the death of someone close to you altered the path your life would take, a critical move that pulled you away from a strong support group only to find yourself in a strange place without any support at all. Maybe a great idea turned flat and was not successful and you experienced ridicule or humiliation.

On the flip side, we've had other situations that were pure genius, pure luck that transformed our lives forever. Have you ever been in the right place at the right time to meet the right person? You meet that special person that changes your life forever - could be your spouse, a backer, the ideal team member that compliments your style and ideas. It could be taking a risk and enrolling in a class that gives you the skill set you lack with a professor willing to help advise and mentor you along the way. Maybe it's entering that pitch competition you thought you didn't have a chance of winning, but you forced yourself to do it for practice if nothing else, and you ended up meeting people that were critical to your continued success. These positive situations, where the adrenaline pumps through your veins and you just know it will turn out, may be significant emotional events for you.

Whether these events have been good or bad, it's how we interpret and internalize the events that determine how we label them; but these significant emotional events changed our life course. For example, let's look at two businesses that started in 2008. Both were in the same industry, real estate, and we all know the market crashed in 2008. Both business owners were impacted but it was how they looked at this critical event, how they interpreted it for their business that made all the difference.

One business chose to adjust, see the event as an unfortunate change in the market, but one that also offered opportunity. Since houses were falling into foreclosure left and right, the opportunity to point customers to these homes to purchase on a short sale or foreclosure basis and still offer them the neighborhood and school district they aspired to, was a boon for the business. Plus, he added personnel to guide potential homeowners through the process of a short sale, attracting many first time buyers looking for a deal, as well as sellers looking for help to maneuver the logistics involved with foreclosure and short sales through their lending institutions. He expanded further and added team members who could help the seller in these unfortunate instances to find housing in rental properties and apartment buildings. This helped to expand the business to property management.

This founder also advised his customers on where to invest in real estate and did some investing himself. Knowing every market, especially real estate, swings like a pendulum, the founder knew the market would come back eventually. He would be ready to sell the properties when indicators showed the market was recovering. In the meantime, he rented them to trustworthy customers he had built relationships with while helping them sell their homes.

This business owner still gave great service and was a real help to buyers and sellers alike. He expanded his territory, specialized in where he saw the market, and in the process made a name for himself as an honest, reliable resource for anyone wanting to buy, sell, rent or have property managed. The business thrived in a market many saw as dead.

The second business owner/founder saw the real estate bust as a bust for his business. He interpreted the crash as a terrible event for his business. He continued to try to do business as usual, the normal functions of selling and buying, assisting with getting traditional mortgages for his clients. But we all know it became a buyer's market and some traditional sellers shied away from putting their home on the market. Instead they were choosing to wait out the market until home prices started to rise. They could afford to do this in the cases where their mortgage rates were good and they were not in a situation where their homes were worth less than what they owed on them.

These were the very people the second business had always targeted and relied on for business. He did not seek out and gain the knowledge needed to help buyers considering a short sale or foreclosure home. In fact, he steered them away from these homes, advising they were too risky an investment. He did not seek out sellers who were looking for a short sale of their property, and did not see them as an opportunity, just too much work.

He did not hire personnel that knew how to work within the system; in fact he let people go. He also shied away from investing in real estate thinking if he put money into a home, there would not be any buyers for the finished product.

His interpretation of the same events as the first business was resoundingly different. He did not see the change in the market as hidden opportunity. The failure to see what could be, to alter his business, change his focus and habits, change his internal identity, resulted in failure of his business. If he had looked at the success of his peer, and mirrored it, he'd be in business today. His interpretation of the events and his negative emotions around them resulted in the closing of his business. He now works for another agency, not his own.

The better we understand the event and our emotion around it, ultimately relates to who our Identity becomes around that event. What we mean by that is that sometimes an emotional event will help us realize what we may be hanging on to; something emotionally that we no longer need. Or, it could help us see what is not really important to us, and help us focus on the things that are important. That 'thing' will be different to each of us; it could be family, success, our spiritual side, our professional life, our life's passion and vocation, etc. As we become more aware of the impact of these events on our lives and our perceptions, we will become more aware of how they shaped who we are – our Identity.

The second way to shape Identity is through conditioning. Conditioning is where you create positive habits, positive behavior patterns. Typically it takes twenty-one days to break a habit.

It has been demonstrated in some of the programs we work with that an individual creates a new habit in the first 21 days and typically between days 36 and 45 that new habit matures and starts to take root. Ultimately, you'll find that when it comes to Identity, if you really want to change your habits, your beliefs and your values, the process will last over a few months and it could be up to a year.

People do this with mental conditioning all the time as well. You start to do something on a regular basis. It could be saving money. It could be eating a certain way. It could be prayer or meditation or something else in the mental realm. It could be getting in the habit of reading. What starts to happen is that you start to create, you start to condition your mind, your body, and your soul, with this new habit and it ultimately changes your Identity.

For me personally, I used conditioning to become a runner! If you knew me eight years ago, I was not a runner. I couldn't run one mile. One day I woke up at the sunny beaches of Miami and said, 'I'm going to run a marathon!'

I started out walking/running a mile and here I am eight years later having completed dozens of races, marathons and triathlons. After a while I built the habits to be able to accomplish my running goals. It was a way to be able to shape my Identity through conditioning, physical conditioning. Our minds work very similarly; the difference is they go to the mental gym.

Think of it this way, we all have a mental gym we can go to and work out. At the mental gym it's like the regular gym, your muscles grow by being pushed beyond their normal capacity and we all expect to be sore after a good workout. With the mental gym we use focus, discipline or the courage to push through and we will get mentally sore - frustrated, discouraged. But you cannot grow or reach any goal without going to the mental gym and facing your roadblock, obstacles - Deception.

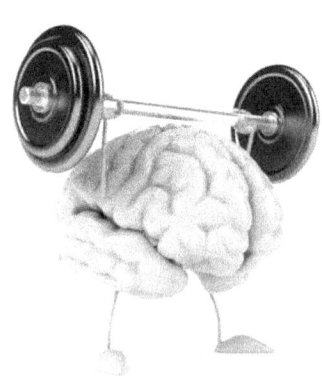

The Mental Gym

The third way to shape your Identity is through your environment.

Have you ever put your feet in the sand on the Ocean or a lake? Have you ever stood at the top of a mountain and stared out over a valley? How did you feel in those places? Those are environments; they evoke a feeling.

Have you heard the saying, 'birds of a feather flock together?' Have you taken a look at the people you hang around with? You are most likely to be like them. That has to do with your environment.

If your mother ever warned you about the gang you hung out with, it's because she knew that you would be seen in the same light as those you associate with; and in that respect she is correct. Take a close look at the people you are with most often; do they offer you insight, wisdom, lessons that you couldn't learn on your own? Are they positive people or do they complain all the time? Do they encourage you or discourage you in your efforts to get your vision? Is their experience at the same level as you? Do they have anything new to contribute to your personal growth, or your Identity? Do they embody the culture you thrive in? The people you spend your time with are part of your environment.

Your business culture is an important part of your Identity as in any other environment. Many business cultures may have the outward semblances of an easygoing, creative, empowering business. You've seen them with the impressive modern furniture, wonderful lighting, pool tables and games, open spaces and community feel. Many firms fit this empowering culture. Others have the outwardly appearance, but foster an interior culture that doesn't mirror the outward appearance. Instead, they are hard driving, demanding, dictating entities without opportunity for all voices to be heard and respected, and often time without real direction or leadership. These types of business culture environments impact our identity too.

That is why it is important to understand the culture you want to create in your business.

Have you ever noticed that certain environments you walk into make you feel a certain way? They can get you excited, sometimes other places you walk into bring you down and you drag a little bit. That's okay too, that is just the environment.

As you start to pay attention to where you are, you'll get to notice the different environments. We all have different environments in our lives - our personal as well as professional lives. Maybe it's where you work out, or where you go enjoy dinners, or spend times with your friends.

One exercise I like to do is to have entrepreneurs take the group of friends they spend the most time with and ask them to identify what they do and how much they make - usually this is a direct reflection on where they are at or where they are going. This is also a great exercise to do with team members, especially in the sales or business development role. It is important to network, to attend seminars and conferences where you can meet people that will elevate you, your skills, your knowledge and finally, your Identity.

In our workday we also have those same things. Do you have a window in your office or do you happen to work in different locations or work outdoors? How does that make you feel?

For me it's better to look at a window than a wall, no matter what art is displayed. It makes me feel good. Do you find places that invigorate you? Where you are, and how it makes you feel also helps to create your Identity as well. The places you put yourself in, the people you associate with, are all a part of your environment and have an impact on your Identity. For example there are many co-work spaces that welcome entrepreneurs and if you are just starting out, they are a good place to hang your hat.

As an entrepreneur when you look to certain co-work spaces, incubators and accelerators, they provide you an environment too. Before choosing one, look at their track record; look at the types of companies they have worked with and what they have gone on to do. Listen to the people who have gone through the programs offered to hear the benefits they received. One of the key reasons to participate in one of these environments is to learn from other businesses what they did when they encountered similar obstacles you may encounter.

For example, the incubator Y Combinator has funded 800 startups since 2005 with a community of 1600 founders and its companies have a combined valuation of over $30 billion. They started with just 8 companies. They focus on first time entrepreneurs. The incubator was formed to make it easier to start a startup. They have well known successes such as Airbnb, Stripe and Dropbox to name a few. The true value they bring to a start up is the mentoring and extensive network of founders, partners and investors.

Tech Stars, another leader in accelerators, has had a total of 517 companies currently active, with an additional 77 acquired, and 66 that failed to pass the program. Tech Stars has an advantage in that the 'classes' are held in different locations globally, so there is likely to be one in your area. The average funding per company is $3,147,629. Again, the value is the mentoring as well as their network.

Before deciding on an incubator or accelerator, consider the makeup of the network and its success rates. Find one that will understand your industry, but is diverse enough to offer you different peer points of view. Remember, this environment, a co-work space, will influence your identity, so it is important that it is aligned with the identity and the outcomes you desire.

Remember, the Identity Model states you can shape your Identity through significant emotional events, conditioning and through your environment. Because Identity is one of the strongest forces of nature, it is very important for you pay attention to how you respond and internalize the three ways your Identity is shaped. You can put your best face forward by learning how to shape your Identity through the good habits, strong beliefs and values you embrace. Now when we refer to the Identity of an Entrepreneur, you have the basic background on why we believe it is so important.

Working with the ESCAPIST ENTREPRENEUR

Case Study: *Escapist Knows Best!*

During my career, I've worked with multiple creative agencies that provided different services; branding, marketing, Public Relations (PR) and even Social Media. The founders and owners of these agencies had one thing in common; they were very creative. They could communicate with images, illustrations, written copy and in 140-character messaging. Their expertise in the creative space was never in doubt. In fact, many won awards for their work, were featured in publications and participated as industry experts on panels.

These clients often had a goal, and in spite of the agency's success, they wanted to grow and get to the next level. The owners/founders understood the need for change in order to grow, but didn't know the 'right' way to get to that level.

The fact was that they were in denial. They would escape into very "busy" activity on the path they finally chose as the 'right' path. They insisted things be done their way, as the only way acceptable, when other ways would garner the same result, maybe even sooner! Because they never wanted to deal with what was really happening in their companies, they could never understand why they didn't grow and reach that next level. Focus is good, but remaining open to other viewpoints, and issues and obstacles you may not be aware of, is critical to be able to pivot and make corrections in your strategies and plans. The Escapists Entrepreneurs running these agencies would not accept any differing viewpoints and strongly defended their position until outside circumstances forced them to change, or at least reconsider outside viewpoints.

They effectively hid their heads in the 'right' path instead of realizing there were other options available; they wore virtual business blinders.

The Escapist is the person that believes if the idea didn't originate with them, it has no value. It is more comfortable to them to escape in busy activity, effectively spinning their wheels, than be open to other's ideas and viewpoints.

Lesson: *Keeping open to other options, viewpoints and guidance, and not being stuck in busy work to prove your way is the only way, will open up opportunities you may have missed to grow and succeed.*

THE IDENTITY OF AN ENTREPRENEUR

Most of our lives we are given titles - Millennials or generation X, business owner, father or mother, sister or brother, investor or even entrepreneur. These titles inevitably become our identity - how we relate to ourselves, the world and in turn how others in the world relate to us. So what is your identity around your life and business? Are you a business owner? A hobbyist? A dreamer? Or are you an entrepreneur?

If you said entrepreneur, then did someone give you this title or is it self-proclaimed? Do you sign up for something? Do you move to a certain city? How did you become an entrepreneur?

As we stated in the previous chapter, the reason identity is so important is that it is the strongest force in human nature. Who we hold ourselves to be will ultimately dictate our future. Said a different way - the person you see yourself as in the mirror is the person you will be today and tomorrow and into the future. So, until you are able to own the Identity of an Entrepreneur, you will most likely struggle in your life with obtaining the ultimate success as an entrepreneur. Ultimately, it is not just the Identity of an Entrepreneur, but rather a successful entrepreneur.

Early in my career, I was embarrassed to be called an entrepreneur; the title of attorney was so much more significant. Not to mention, I had a personal belief that since I did not make the cover of Fast Company or some other prominent publication I didn't have the accolades around my achievements. So despite having founded a multimedia company with operations in multiple states, with over fifty team members and partnership with global brands, I was not an entrepreneur. And when I divested of that project and began consulting law firms with Fortune 200 clients, I was not an entrepreneur. And, even though I have started over 2 dozen companies over the years, I was not an entrepreneur. Most recently, as I have educated, mentored and inspired thousands of entrepreneurs, it began to set in that I just might be an entrepreneur.

When I finally accepted that *being* an entrepreneur is not about doing something or achieving some milestone, I began to understand that anyone, anywhere could be an entrepreneur. After all, entrepreneurialism is a mindset. I began to realize that the successes are just as important as the failures and that the answers I have based on my education, experiences and the great mentorship I received, all led to a complete solution to the entrepreneurial community. It was in this moment that I had the mindset of entrepreneurship.

That mindset is spreading too. According to a recent infographic from oDesk, 71% of those still at "regular" jobs want to quit and be entirely independent. 61% say they are likely to quit within 2 years. That means some of your staff, your team, may want to go out on their own, and soon. If they are a Millennial, 58% of them already classify themselves as entrepreneurs. This isn't necessarily a bad thing if they have the mindset, and you have an entrepreneurial culture. They can contribute greatly and when they choose to leave, you will have another entrepreneur peer.

Their reasons for wanting to become an entrepreneur probably mirror yours: working wherever, whenever, on things that interest them, and so they can travel while they work. Many of the new entrepreneurs are freelancers, and 21% of them are still in College!

Once I realized that most of my life experiences, daily choices and most importantly my mindset were growth oriented, focused on empowerment and were sprinkled with uncertainty, I began to realize that I was being entrepreneurial.

I believe that **being** an entrepreneur is like **being** happy or **being** caring. These examples are states of beings and people take action within these states of beings. Similarly, being an entrepreneur is similar and being a successful entrepreneur requires being of a certain mindset and having certain habits, behaviors and patterns.

One thing that is important to note is that a title is just that, a title. So, until you face the distractions surrounding a business, overcome obstacles and deal with deception, one may not want the title of entrepreneur.

The ability to deal with uncertainty, and the ability to overcome deception is the essence of being an entrepreneur. Being an entrepreneur is not a 'to do' list. It's dealing with the other, more sinister obstacles and distractions that we face each day. The distractions that come from within – fear, doubt, negative self talk, no belief that you can hold you back from the success you desire in your business, idea or service. As the leader/ business owner, these internally based distractions will permeate your business, trickle down to your team, and soon they will mirror the same fear, doubt and negativity.

Without the internal compass that consists of the good habits, positive attitude and clear focus to take you through the fear, restore your confidence and destroy doubt, you will forever struggle as the Distracted Entrepreneur instead of obtaining the successful entrepreneur hallmark of moving into the Identity of an Entrepreneur.

Whatever identity you hold onto, it affects your ability to be successful.

What is an Entrepreneur?

In the past an entrepreneur was someone who started a business, any business. For the purposes of this book, an entrepreneur is more than someone who owns a business. They are pioneers, they are risk takers, they are disruptive and they are focused on being change agents in their lives. You see, in recent times, there's been a paradigm shift that an entrepreneur is a startup, a small business, a new entrepreneur, an artist, a musician, an inventor, a non-profit, and a serial entrepreneur. Today, an entrepreneur can be anyone, in fact an entrepreneur can work for another company. It's interesting that today 90% of people think an entrepreneur is a *mindset*, and not owning a business.*

As you can see from the oDesk survey, today it is about working when you want to, where you want to, with the freedom to travel and the freedom to work on things that you love and you have a passion for. That's the shift, it's now about being in control of your life, your destiny.

Being an entrepreneur is about that personal power over our own lives. That's a mindset. With a mindset like this, it's not so much about the business; it's more about who you are as an individual. In my experience, an entrepreneur will take the risks to pursue their dreams, usually with little or no money, and are focused on growing personally and professionally. While the business knowledge and strategy are important, it is driven by the ability to execute, to develop and having the right mindset.

The entrepreneur of today still needs to deal with the same things other generations dealt with like sales, staffing, growth and maintaining profitability, only today the mindset is about personal freedoms too. If we melded together someone with sales, leadership and culture we'd have the ultimate example of an entrepreneur. As entrepreneurs surrounding themselves with people who can excel in the areas of knowledge, strategy, and business development, we can create successful teams.

How do you transform into the ultimate you, the ultimate entrepreneur? Through the secrets we've learned working with millionaires and billionaires to achieve their success. Using these secrets to transform into the Identity of an Entrepreneur, instead of just having the title is key.

What does it mean to have the Identity of an Entrepreneur? We've talked about the importance of Identity and what it really means in our professional lives. How our past can influence our present and that it can be changed. What we mean by the Identity of an Entrepreneur is that the Entrepreneur has certain characteristics they exhibit that make up who they are and how they do business. These are the same characteristics millionaires and billionaires excel in, or their team members excel in, and through these characteristics they are able to easily move through the Cycle of Growth and transform to *being* an Entrepreneur, having the Identity of an Entrepreneur.

The next chapter goes over the key areas to excel in and how you can transform into having the Identity of an Entrepreneur.

Identity of an Entrepreneur is:

Development of certain characteristics that are beneficial or necessary in order to push through the hurdles of having your own business.
*It is an **<u>Attitude</u>** or **<u>Way of Being.</u>***

Working with the FEAR-SEEKER ENTREPRENEUR

Case Study: *I'm afraid!*

Entrepreneurs that are Fear Seekers tend to be interesting, in that they are always seeking security and certainty, and there really isn't any as an entrepreneur. In fact, there is one guarantee as an entrepreneur; the more you have to risk the more you stand to gain. Ultimate growth comes from our ability to take risks.

I worked with a very successful national company that had been in business for almost three decades with hundreds of employees. They decided to move the business online and create technology automation in their business and monetize it as an additional revenue stream. In my opinion, this move was not made from a place of possibility and abundance, but rather it was made from a place of scarcity.

Unfortunately, a transition of this kind is fraught with obstacles and problems. The company didn't want to deal with the fact that their company wasn't ready to make such a transition; their sales force was struggling with the new technology advances and pushed back to management. Much of the decision making process was around the opinions of the staff, who all wanted security, as opposed to what was good for the growth and longevity of the business. The security they sought was really fear of the change. This transition was pushed on the staff as opposed to created and developed by the team.

All decisions were made out of fear and scarcity. The managers looked for security and certainty for the staff, but in the technology space, those are rare commodities. They wanted to build in a cushion, a comfort zone that was never going to manifest. Even the funding strategy was focused on security.

If they had accepted that the transition needed to be made, and made it, they would have pushed through the Deception phase. Instead, when it became uncomfortable – when they reached Deception – they ended up quitting on the project after multiple years and a great deal of money and resources that were already into the project. The management was afraid to alienate or lose the staff rather than go through the transition to grow to the next level and replace staff if necessary. They ended up saying, "it would not work" for their industry.

Today, that industry has all but moved to technology-based automation! They effectively stepped back, based on a fear of lack of security effectively losing what would have been a firm foothold on the next generation of their industry. Instead of being the Industry leader, they were the follower. An interesting note is that I recently met with this enterprise and they have continued to grow through acquisition. So by society's standards, they are successful financially.

Lesson: *Uncertainty and insecurity are part of any business cycle, especially one in growth mode. Understanding the cycle, and where the business and staff are in relation to the cycle is key to pushing through, putting in place strategies to assist in overcoming the obstacles that arise in any transition.*

THE CYCLE OF GROWTH

Successful entrepreneurs are known for setting goals and working to achieve those goals. The laser focus, the drive to produce results is what successful entrepreneurs are all about.

Yet, sometimes we hit roadblocks, obstacles and struggle to achieve those goals. Many entrepreneurs ask why this is, how they overcome it and what can be done differently. A foundational model we use - the Cycle of Growth- helps explain this. The Cycle of Growth is adapted from Rod Hairston's book, ***Are You Up For The Challenge***.

The Cycle of Growth is a roadmap for change and growth – to help all Entrepreneurs to reach their goals and achieve success. Throughout this book we will be referring to the different phases of the Cycle of Growth, so it's important that we introduce you to the cycle and that you understand how it will help you to transform to the Identity of an Entrepreneur.

As entrepreneurs, we're already committed to the journey, the adventure. Having an idea of what will come along your path will help you to get to your end goal. There are set phases you will go through and we'll help you get through them.

Knowing what phase of the cycle you are in, and the process for moving through it successfully will be the key to reaching the end – the vision you started with.

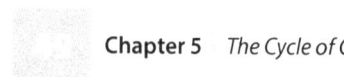

There are 4 phases in The Cycle of Growth:

1. *INCEPTION*
2. *DECEPTION*
3. *TRANSITION*
4. *IDENTITY*

The best way to understand the Cycle of Growth is to visually see it at work.

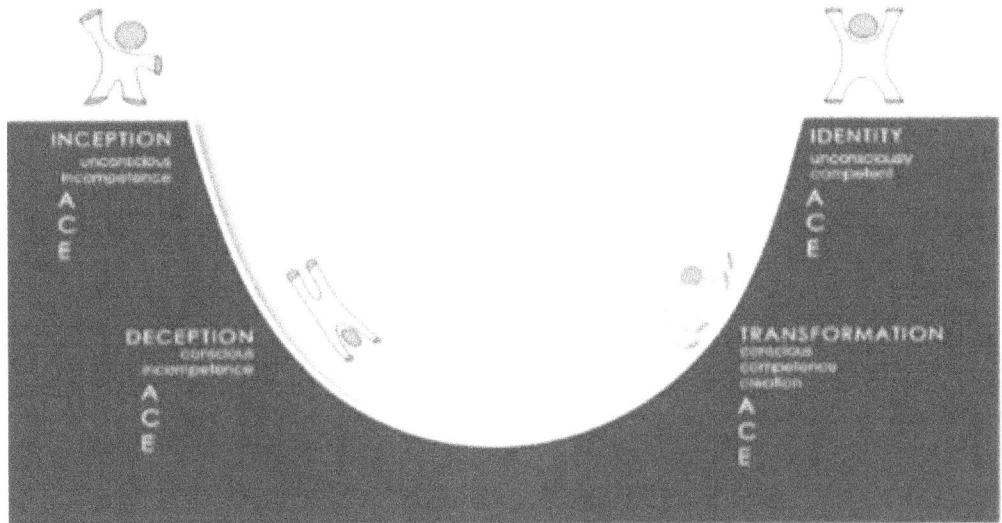

We start in Inception and usually all we can see is Identity, the vision of what we see can become our reality.

Have you ever heard someone say "I have an app that will get a million downloads" or "Everyone loves my cooking" or "I have a new formula that will revolutionize the industry"? While these may seem true and are totally possible, there is a journey to get there that involves many steps and obstacles that must be overcome.

In our model, you will see under the phase name A, C and E. These stand for the Attitude, Competence, and Energy. Depending on where you are in the cycle, the levels of these three key factors will vary. We'll talk about these factors as we discuss each phase.

The next step is where the obstacles come up - this is what we call Deception. You know you've heard of famous obstacles like the number of shots Michael Jordan took, and missed, the number of times a successful entrepreneur was rejected for funding (Starbucks was rejected 242 times) or the obstacles that resulted in the thousands of models of the Dyson vacuum cleaner before it became successful. These were obstacles and you may even have examples in your own business.

The bottom line is that as entrepreneurs we are going to "fall down." There are going to be times when things come up. In these moments of facing obstacles, how do you react? How do you respond? Where is your mindset? How you respond, how you handle them is the Deception you experience in your mind. It is at this time that you are unconsciously incompetent - you don't know what you do not know. It is at this point that an entrepreneur will typically go to one of seven places as they deal with these obstacles. (We will dive into these in detail later).

It is important to note (and if you do not take anything else from this book, take this one thing) - **deception is going to happen and the more you welcome it, the better off you are going to be.**

You see the Cycle of Growth for an entrepreneur is a lot like going to the gym. As an entrepreneur there are plenty of strategic and tactical resources available to you, just like there are plenty of workout routines and gym programs that you can participate in to get the desired results. So what makes the difference between the in shape people and the out of shape people? From the people who finish the program and do not? Their mental toughness - did they go to the mental gym?

As we've discussed in previous chapters, the mental gym is where you go to strengthen your mental muscles, where you go to work through the soreness of overcoming obstacles, where the muscles get sore in the face of frustration, rejection and uncertainty. It is at the mental gym where success is trained for and journeys are won.

When an entrepreneur begins to embrace deception and the mental gym, they will move into the third phase called "Transformation." This is where entrepreneurs become creative and begin to move to the next level.

As an entrepreneur goes through this phase they strengthen the mental muscle, they build the characteristics necessary for success. It is through this process they obtain the identity they set out for in the first place.

Identity is the place they envision from the beginning - it is where they set their sites on during Inception. These are the types of things that you see in an entrepreneur's vision board, it is what they talk about over coffee and fantasize about over drinks after a long week of grinding. The good news is that anything you set your mind to is possible - it's just a matter of doing the work.

Let's take a deep dive into each of the phases in the next few pages . . .

The first phase of the Cycle of Growth is the Inception Phase. This is the phase when you start anything new. In this phase, you don't know what you don't know yet. Your attitude is super high, your confidence level isn't there yet, but your effort is typically really high.

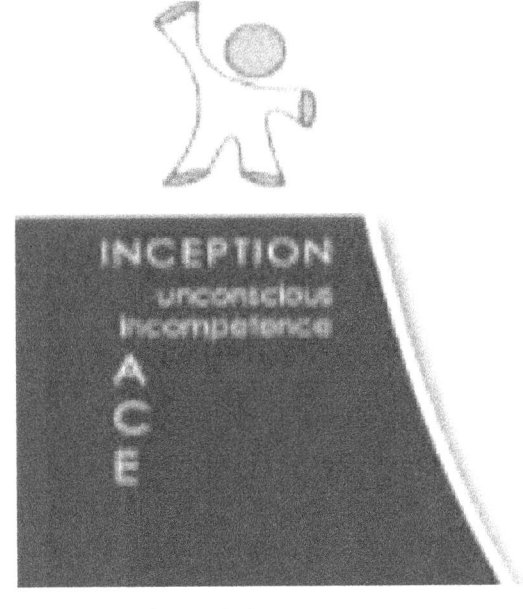

You see what you want, very clearly. There's a lot of emotion around it - you're excited! There is leverage and purpose to why you want to do start something. You can identity with it because it feels real to you as if you can just reach out and touch it.

The heightened awareness and excitement is the Inception Phase – the first part of the Cycle of Growth. This phase is transitional. You can't stay in this phase very long. Emotion and energy wanes, distractions take away your focus and your energy, you may become a 'Distracted Entrepreneur.' Life comes along and you have to address it.

In this phase your A (attitude) is high, your C (competency) is not here yet, but you don't know it, so it feels high too. Your E (energy) is high too with the start of this new idea.

After the initial emotion surrounding your goal ebbs, the next phase is 'Deception.' Your attitude is challenged; your competency isn't there yet because it is still something new for you and you are still learning and adjusting. (Getting the business knowledge you need to succeed.) Your effort is also challenged.

This phase is also referred to as *Conscious Incompetence* - you now know what you don't know and it doesn't feel good. It *never* feels good. No one likes to feel incompetent in what they are doing, especially when you started out so happy, so sure of yourself. Your actions and thoughts around the goal are not automatic yet, but will be when you reach your goal.

Until it's automatic and second nature to you, you'll have to go through this phase. While this phase is hard, you will really *want* to go through it.

You want the pain and uncertainty that comes in this phase. Really you do!

That uncomfortable feeling, that tightness in your gut, dry mouth, and insomnia are a part of the Deception Phase. Deception signals change. It signals work and discomfort and stress, we won't deny that, but it is essential to go through it, feel what it is to you, and get to the other side of it in order to become successful.

Yes, there is an 'other side' to this phase.

Many entrepreneurs stall at this phase; they become too uncomfortable and quit, or focus their energy on other things forgetting the great idea, the vision they had at the beginning. If they only pushed through, if they only focused, they could move through to success.

Seth Godin, in his book **The Dip** talks about pushing through the dip, the discomfort to the reward on the other side. "Short-term pain has more impact on most people than long-term benefits do, which is why it's so important for you to amplify the long-term benefits of not quitting." We happen to agree with this statement and stress that you have to look at the end game – your goal. If it's something worth doing, then stick with it. If not, then reevaluate and put your efforts on a better goal.

Most entrepreneurs experience this with their idea, the vision they see for their company or product or app. They can see it and are excited because they know it is real and can be done.

During this phase you learn and research and work very hard. This is the phase where doubt seeps in, uncertainty is a bedfellow, and you wonder if your efforts are really worth it.

At the end of Deception is the place where you've gone through the discomfort; you've learned what you needed to learn, you have new perspective – you're ready! When that discomfort is gone and replaced with certainty – you know you've moved out of Deception into the next phase.

In this phase your A (attitude) is not the best, so it is low, your C (competency) is better, you are at least aware of what you don't know and need to know and your E (energy) is hard to keep up, it is low.

Transformation is the phase where you are recommitted to your goal, your vision. You are consciously competent in what you are doing, you are still feeling your way through and you may still realize some discomfort, but not as much as in the Deception phase – and that's okay!

You are armed with support; the knowledge and tools you need, you've researched the right things, you are focused on what really needs your attention, and you understand the 'Why' of what you are doing.

Remember, when an entrepreneur begins to condition their mind in the mental gym, they will move into and through this phase.

As an entrepreneur goes through this phase they strengthen the mental muscle,

they build the characteristics necessary for success. It is through this process they obtain the identity they set out for in the first place.

It all starts to align. You've established focus and habits you need to focus on to reach your goals. The more you become consistent, the more your actions become a habit, that's where you move into the last phase – Identity.

In this phase your A (attitude) is much better, yet you may still struggle. Your C (competency) is high, you are consciously competent and getting comfortable again in your knowledge base, your E (energy) is recovering, your excitement is coming back!

Phase Four: Identity

The Identity phase is really the fun phase. You are unconsciously competent; it's easy for you, you look good and you feel good doing what you do, you are totally confident and carry yourself with a presence of confidence. In this phase you do things automatically, without having to stop and think about them. People are drawn to you, to your energy. Things start to happen for you.

Attitude is high, or neutral, which is okay too. Your confidence is high and your

effort is there because that is WHO you are now! If we were to outline your A, C and E it would be that all three are at a high level.

This process is the overarching process we'll be covering in detail in this book. We will get you to the Identity of an Entrepreneur – not just the title.

The four phases should be familiar to any entrepreneur if they made it through the Deception phase. If not, this book will help you recognize the uncertainty in that phase, help you focus and create new, useful habits that you will use as you move forward in the Identity of an Entrepreneur.

This cycle is true for any goal you want to reach; working out, eating right, helping your kids set and achieve goals. Remember, as you go through the cycle, it is a cycle and one you can move easily through each phase by learning the right mindset, having the right habits, attitude and focus. We cover these more in upcoming chapters.

This is the model for creating Identity, so reaching any goal, creating a result comes from your beliefs, your Identity.

WHAT TYPE OF ENTREPRENEUR ARE YOU?

There are different types of Entrepreneurs, just like there are many types of people and there are diverse groups who have classified or categorized entrepreneurs in an effort to "deal with them." What I have found is that we are all unique beings who happen to be wired similarly and so ultimately, we tend to have similar habits, patterns and behaviors. These similarities can be grouped together to create styles or characteristics upon which we can begin to delineate entrepreneurs.

The importance around understanding what style you exhibit helps to handle issues as they come up and how you interact with people. Knowing and understanding these styles, and how to break out of habits that put you into the negative aspects of these styles, will help you in many ways. For example, most of us are familiar with the Competitive Style, where the person likes to be a winner and in some cases can be very aggressive. Knowing you are dealing with a person with a competitive style you can adjust how you deal with them, and make the outcome of the encounter a win for them.

Another benefit of understanding your style is the ability to better relate to what motivates you, how you handle risk and why and how you will be able to connect with others and their style. You will know how to interact, to diffuse a situation, or welcome someone into your team with a complementary style. Becoming a strong leader and understanding how to work within your style and others as an entrepreneur will allow you to meet others where they are at and create collaborative win-win situations in your business endeavors.

No style is wrong or bad and we all exhibit some characteristics of each style depending on the situation, and our current mindset. And that's great, in fact, there are times you will want to take on the characteristics of each of the styles depending on the situation, the players involved and the outcome desired. Recognizing the different styles in others allows you to put a game plan in place for taking action. Understanding what style you use most often and what style complements yours could be your key to success!

Before looking into the different style of Entrepreneurs, let's look at key factors of Risk, Motivation and Focus. These are found in each style, so it is important to go over them before diving into the styles of Entrepreneurs.

How much risk are you comfortable taking with your company?

Your willingness to take an intelligent risk is directly proportional to your ability to deal with uncertainty. The more you are comfortable with change and uncertainty, the more you are willing to take a risk. If you are cautious and looking for certainty, then you most likely are risk averse.

Both extremes are important to understand because a balance is the best of both worlds. You won't be so overly optimistic as to ignore the reality of current situations and you won't be so mired in certainty that you refuse to compromise and stifle the growth of your company.

That's why we use the term 'intelligent risk.' Using your team and their expertise, along with your own to evaluate risks is essential to growth. Knowing your comfort level and the pitfalls that can come by being stuck in any one style will help you to take the necessary steps – risks – to grow your company.

What makes you get up in the morning and gets you out of bed?

As an entrepreneur, you are focused on success, on making it. But what is your motivation? We can be internally motivated, externally motivated, or have a balance of both. No one way is right or wrong, but understanding your motivation and your team's will make managing expectations and your team easier for you.

Looking for approval or validation from an outside source rather than from your own self is External Motivation. While an external motivation can take an entrepreneur so far - they will find the energy, the perseverance to overcome obstacles and can achieve some levels of success, however, at some point, this motivation may not be enough to continue to grow and move into uncertainty to create the ultimate growth and success desired. When an entrepreneur relies on external motivation to get results their path is always in flux. Their days are good or bad based on the external motivation that they receive. The control lies in others and not in the Entrepreneur.

Internal Motivation comes from within. Understanding self worth and being driven by a desire to succeed, for reasons known only to you, is Internal Motivation. You may be committed to external results, but the reason you get up in the morning is not for others, necessarily, but for you. The reason could be a drive to succeed to have means to travel, be generous to friends and family, to make your family and mentors right to believe in you, that you did become a success! It could be that you are in an industry you know is mired in in the technology of the past and you want to change the industry, set a new standard. Perhaps you want to make a difference in the lives of the less fortunate, make a difference to the entire world.

Internal motivation is a constant force in your life when creating your future. Your motivation doesn't depend on others but rather on yourself and your focus on why you are doing what you do. What is your motivation?

A balance between internal and external motivators is ideal. That balance, coupled with the balance of focus on yourself and others is the start of the makings of a visionary leader.

Focus

Where is your focus?

There are 4 Laws of Focus and they are covered in detail in chapter two, Creating Focus in the Life of an Entrepreneur. Let's recap so it is top of mind.

The 4 Laws are:

1. **WHAT YOU FOCUS ON YOU FIND**

2.   *WHAT YOU FOCUS ON SEEMS REAL*

3.   *WHAT YOU FOCUS ON WILL GROW*

4.   *WHAT YOU FOCUS ON YOU BECOME*

We cannot emphasize enough that a key aspect to success is focus. We discuss it in detail in this book because it is so important to attaining your vision, your dream. It's easy to get sidetracked with life and the different Entrepreneur Styles have different areas of focus. Knowing these different styles, and their focus, will help you recognize when you are too deep in the details and too distracted to make a difference.

Focus is one of the key ways to strengthen yourself at the mental gym. The ability to face adversity, to break through obstacles and overcome frustration all come from dealing with deception and a strong focus.

Similar to motivation, an entrepreneur can be focused externally (on others) or internally (the self) or have a balance. As we go through the eight different Entrepreneur Styles, note which focus area you are at, as well as your team. If you find that the focus is not on your core competencies, not on the things that will help grow your business, determine what style would work best to shift the focus to the business goals. Again, as you begin to understand this in more detail, you can build your strength as a leader in becoming better at meeting people where they are at and also understanding how to coach and mentor into success.

Many people are motivated by others' needs and a strong desire to be liked. If you like people and feel you are focused on other's needs, yet have your own reasons to get up in the morning – a balanced motivation – we call this style Social.

This entrepreneur we all know; they are always positive, always happy, warm and outgoing. You love to have them on your team because they understand the shared dynamics and are not looking for personal accolades as much as the acknowledgement of the group's accomplishments to the outside world, so long as the group acknowledges their contribution. They are also very adept at convincing others to see their point of view. They are fun, intelligent and easy to get along with and they work hard to establish and nurture relationships. Having characteristics of the Social Style can be very useful when fundraising; the needed enthusiasm and knowledge to secure funding and support is exhibited. However, because they are so eager to be liked, they are limited. They will lean toward pleasing others instead of rocking the boat or doing what is right for the company or venture, limiting its growth potential.

Style: Competitive

The entrepreneur that exhibits the Competitive Style is internally motivated. This Entrepreneur looks, acts and is successful; no matter what stage of business they are in they appear to everyone as a success. And indeed they are successful! These are the hustlers, the monitizers of ideas and businesses; they appear fearless to the outside world. They are extremely focused on what they want to accomplish and little will distract them from their vision.

Most entrepreneurs have some of this characteristic style and use it well. The down side of the Competitive Style is that there is the 'winning at all costs' attitude that results in alienating others. It also can result in the absolute of win-lose instead of negotiate and compromise. While being competitive is an asset in many instances, if it is taken to the extreme it could result in a breakdown of the team, and desertion of key team members.

Style: Empowering

The entrepreneurs that exhibit the style of Empowering are just that; they are very concerned for others, they want to nurture and help others develop and grow. Entrepreneurs comfortable in this style exhibit empathy, tolerance and can be very generous with their time and expertise since they give value and support in exchange for their money and support – to them a 'win-win' proposition. This style can also invest in things that cost more than their potential return and while wonderful as the investor in your venture, it may not be the greatest attribute when trying to run lean and mean.

Style: Compliant

The flip side of the Empowering Style of entrepreneur is the Compliant Style. While totally focused externally on others, they are typically tactically focused. Don't look to them for the great marketing idea; rather look to them to execute it flawlessly. They are not comfortable with taking risks; they are steady and reliable workers. They are not able to sell your product, service or idea, but they will take the order with precision. They can be overwhelmed easily and are the worrier in the team. It's good to have someone who is concerned for the enterprise and to have someone you can rely on to get the details right, so this is not necessarily something you want to avoid in a team member. This style is important to your team, as they will keep things orderly and moving forward.

Style: Aggressive

The Aggressive Style Entrepreneur is externally motivated, but internally focused. Typically they plow ahead not seeing or listening to any obstacle in their way. They tend to be forceful and controlling, even combative with team members or subordinates. Sometimes these characteristics are needed to shake up an organization and pull it out of the mud it is stuck in. They tend to push strongly, but they really are looking out for their own interests, and if this person owns the company, that could be the driving force to success.

This Entrepreneur style is politically savvy; they are calculating and very perceptive of the cultural shifts in the company and position themselves to take advantage and control. When an organization is paralyzed, this style, or some of its characteristics are needed, if not welcome.

Style: Driven

Sometimes the Driven Style of Entrepreneur is confused with the Aggressive style. A Driven Entrepreneur is both internally focused and internally motivated. They usually exhibit high levels of energy and look for new ways of doing things. They are focused on getting results and expect their team to also focus on the same results, with the same intensity.

They have the characteristics of persistence, resourcefulness, tenaciousness and exceptional focus. They often stumble through and don't always get along well with others. They come off as abrasive and sometimes arrogant in their persistence to achieve results.

This style is forceful, and results oriented. When a team is floundering, working very hard but little to show for it, the Driven characteristics - that focus on getting results – can be effective in guiding the team to the desired results. The caution with this style is not to overrun the team, insult them, or burn them out in the blind effort to produce results.

Style: Cautious

Speaking of caution, the Cautious Style of Entrepreneur, while focused on others and externally motivated, can be rigid and uncompromising. This Style works best in organizations that have spelled out the rules and policies so they know what to do, exactly. In a start up organization this is good to have if you are developing or working with formulas, chemistry and manufacturing specifications – areas where following specific steps and methodology are critical to success. There are many industries where the rigidity and uncompromising nature of the Cautious Style is not only welcome, but also expected.

While they are uncomfortable in environments with rapid change and adaptation, we argue that they are very much needed in this space. This style team member is loyal, dependable and will politely point out the problems they see before you will see them; they will politely challenge the proposed changes.

They are also conformists; you won't see them dying their hair blue unless the entire office shows up in blue hair. They want certainty and assurance that the company will be around for awhile, that they can settle in and complete the processes that give them that reassurance.

Style: Visionary

Every Entrepreneur has some characteristics of the Visionary Style. This entrepreneur is internally motivated and has balanced their focus to others and self. They are committed to what they are doing fully and have a total belief in their product, service or company. They can see the future as they know they can create it; one that is exciting for them. They are motivated by an innate desire to expand their horizons, to explore the unknown.

It isn't only their vision that propels them forward; others get behind the visionary because the excitement and enthusiasm they hold is contagious. They have the ability to light that same excitement in the people around them. What others think is impossible, they believe and can execute to make it possible.

The Visionary is critical to any organization, from an established company to a start up. Without the belief in what the future will hold, a company risks falling into complacency, and can turn into a follower in its industry rather than being the pioneer every other company is scrambling to catch up to.

The downside of the Visionary is that they tend to downplay risks because of their strong beliefs. They are risk takers and should rely on their team to help them keep the reality of where the firm is currently, so the risks they take are 'intelligent risks.' These entrepreneurs are comfortable in uncertainty and have mastered how to easily move through Deception (uncertainty) into Transformation. The team under this type of Entrepreneur will learn a great deal as they flow from one stage of the Cycle of Growth easily into the next.

Understanding where you are in the mix of styles will help you understand the responses you get from your peers, subordinates and everyone you meet, in all situations. A mix of these Styles and motivations is ideal, and recognizing when we are holding back to be liked or running over people to win can change the dynamics and culture of an organization in a flash. Responding to situations rather than reacting to them, keeping the different styles in mind will help to make any environment easier to maneuver (including with investors, lenders, employees, vendors, manufacturers and competitors).

THE FUNDING MYTH

Funding is the fuel to keep the engine going. At the end of the day, whether you need it or not, everyone feels they need more money. That's okay, that's a good place. Many entrepreneurs feel that way; I feel that way, my clients feel that way, we all are looking for additional funds. That's why understanding this is so important. You need to test things out, expand your company, that's where funding comes in.

But how do you find the RIGHT investor?

Do you know what to do to prepare for those investor meetings? Do you know how to close the deal? These are key questions that we will answer.

Based on our experience with millionaires and billionaires we realized what you need to do and what you need to present to get funded. We've developed a system that we know you will benefit from process based on these secrets. We've raised tens of millions of dollars for ourselves and for other entrepreneurs. These are the ideals they talk about to achieving success and what they are looking for as well.

When you are getting ready to make successful investing presentations, most successful entrepreneurs demonstrate that they or their team excel in Business Knowledge, Business Strategy, Business Development, Mindset and Behavior. They are able to show they have an understanding, not only in their presentation to the investors, but also the way they operate, the people they connect with in the type of business they are doing. They demonstrate that they excel in those four areas.

Most of these people excel in certain areas, or have a team that excels in these areas. Investors want to know that the person presenting to them, or their team, has these characteristics. These four areas are covered later in the book, but are key to successfully meeting and convincing investors you are ready to take their money.

Another intangible is that the investors are betting on YOU, the entrepreneur and are asking themselves if they will get a return on their investment. Many times, whether the potential investor(s) are doing it at a conscious level or unconscious level, they are analyzing, judging and vetting and are looking and asking, 'can this entrepreneur group create the outcomes they are saying?'

They are also asking, 'do they have the beliefs necessary to produce that success? Can they create effective habits on a repetitive basis to really move the needle for their business? Are they focused? Can they deal with obstacles, the uncertainty, and the valley of doubt every entrepreneurial organization is going to go through?

They are looking at the four characteristics. We talk about the Identity of an Entrepreneur, the 7 Obstacles an Entrepreneur faces, habit and mindset and focus. These are critical to understand before you jump into securing funding. The Funding Myth is when we hear entrepreneurs say that all they need is money to succeed. We've found that without demonstrating these characteristics and ability to succeed, funding will remain elusive.

This funding journey is one that many entrepreneurs embark on, and few succeed. 90% of all small business fail within five years with the leading cause being lack of capital. In an effort to increase the levels of success let's break it down into the simple secrets, what does it really take.

To start with the most important aspect is having the right mindset - an entrepreneur must be ready "with the right thinking" to start on the journey. This mindset involves a lot of uncertainty and the ability to move into uncharted and often uncomfortable waters.

Often an entrepreneur will need to have the knowledge to make the presentation and to be able to speak about the opportunity. This often requires focused research and a well-practiced presentation. Also, it is important to understand the amount of time that goes into these efforts - fundraising can often be a full time job. Additionally, the ability to deal with rejection around the asking process is essential. Since typically the first "round of asking" is to family and friends you have to feel comfortable in that arena...or push through the discomfort and make the ask anyway.

Focus is so important we've devoted a chapter to it. When fundraising, remain focused. Remember, oftentimes you're going to get NO's before you get YES. If that scares you, if that's something you aren't comfortable with, that's okay. There are many entrepreneurs who got rejected and went on to lead great companies.

One example is Starbucks. They were rejected 242 times by banks for funding. If they had not pushed through that 243rd time, there would not be Starbucks as we know it today. It would still be a great company, but it never would have grown to where it is today without that focus. It took being focused on the vision; it took being focused on the future, even after every rejection. They stayed focused long after it became uncomfortable to be focused.

Understand going into fundraising is a full time job, in addition to being the entrepreneur, the leader. It is difficult. There are going to be additional efforts that are required. Trying to juggle running your business, growing your business, keeping all the balls in the air, and then raising funds on top of it all is difficult, but not impossible. So in addition to being faced with selling your product or services, now you are selling to investors too! It takes a lot of work and resources, many ups and downs. This can be part of the process, so your mindset and focus, if aligned with your vision, can serve you well during this process.

Sometimes you may get a YES that doesn't pan out, other times, the YES is real. Be focused on what you really want, the why – not the money, but the *why* of what you are looking for; your goal.

Stay focused because it's easy to get distracted, but know, until the investors have signed the documents and the money is in the bank, it isn't a done deal. Deals can be finalized or fall apart in the 11th hour.

What does that really mean?

Identifying the RIGHT investor is important. Understand that certain people have an appetite for investing. Family & friends are one group.

 *An Angel investor* typically is someone who is removed from you that is an Angel, they swoop in and provide the funding to get things going. Usually the risk is higher at this level. They usually provide initial funding, sometimes called 'seed' funding, but they usually come on early in the process. They may want to see if you've invested your own money, if family and friends have put in money, but not necessarily.

 *Venture Capitalist (VCs)* come next. They want to know if they dump a bunch of fuel on this, a chunk of money on your idea, product, service or business, how do they rapidly grow it, how do they explode this company. Typically there is some type of viable product; and typically there is some model in place that demonstrates revenue.

VCs bring on the next round of funding. Typically a Series A or Series B round of funding. First or second round of funding comes through VCs.

 *Equity Crowdfunding* is an interesting option because it is a mix of family, friends, Angels, and VCs and any one of them. Crowdfunding is mostly used in a Family & Friends round and it is at Angel and VC level where we typically see Equity Crowdfunding. It means they will seek the funding in the same way; they will seek seed for capital, Series A or Series B, but instead of going to their traditional organization, they will go to the crowd of potential investors for their funding.

The Securities and Exchange Commission (SEC) historic vote in 2015 finally opened the door for unaccredited investors to invest directly in companies – securing equity for their investment. This opened the door for individuals to invest regardless of their income level and created a huge pool of investors for companies wanting to give up equity.

 The next level is Private Equity. Typically at this level investors are buying and selling of companies. So they are looking to buy equity in multiple shares from a company and then sell it. They are coming in from a funding source or will come in and say 'you have a good platform; we'll give you money to grow or acquire other existing entities.' These investors are not typically looking at startups, but are looking to grow, either through building a company, maximizing the revenue, or through a platform and acquiring them.

 Traditionally lending is through a typical bank with Micro Loans, Small Business Administration Loans (SBA), Real Estate loans, or Line of Credit. They will give you some type of loan, or line or credit or factoring that goes along with traditional form of lending.

When you understand what stage of funding your business is in, you will start to identify the right audience. You want to find an audience that wants to listen to you. Who's the audience looking for a deal like yours? What's great is you can even get online and use resources to find out not only the different level of these investors, but what is their appetite.

For example, if you are making money and want to grow your business, you probably want to look into VC funding. So look at your industry first and the different funding sources existing that invest in your industry. Instead of a mass approach to a thousand people you don't know, you can laser focus in on the ones that fund your kind of deal in your industry. Use your focus and resources in connecting with them.

Remember, is it so important to get an introduction whenever possible. Randomly you can meet your investor in an elevator, it has happened, but a warm introduction goes a long way. If you ask someone to make an introduction, sometimes they will say yes and sometimes they will say no. If they say yes, understand they are putting their stamp of approval on the introduction.

Part of who you are, and being able to demonstrate having the characteristics we mentioned earlier in this chapter, will make people want to make the introduction for you. They will want to see you succeed and to get the investments you need, they will want to make those introductions.
It is very important that you seek out getting peer introductions and peer recommendation for a warm introduction. It makes all the difference to Investors.

Once you know whom to meet with for your investment, what's next?

When you meet with an investor, it's important to tell a story, and have a story line. It's important to tell the right story with the right slides in your presentation. There is nothing worse than not having the right presentation. We've had experience with one group where we asked them to send us their deck to review a day or two before the meeting. They sent a seventy three-page PowerPoint presentation. With only thirty minutes for the investor meeting, that's less than thirty seconds per slide. Knowing we would not move that quickly, we narrowed the presentation down to the key points.

As investors become more sophisticated and as you talk to the bigger investors of the world they tell us they are getting thousands and thousands of pitches. They already know the questions they are going to ask, they already know what they are looking for, so if your presentation can answer those questions up front, you've gotten past that first filter, you've gotten past that first vetting. That's why the right presentation telling the right story is so important. As the entrepreneur, we know you have a great deal to share with the investor, but they already know what they are looking for and if you can tell them what they are looking for in your first presentation, you will pass the muster and get to the next level.

The presentation should be focused on only what the investors want to know: who you are, your management team, what market are you in and what are the numbers in that market, what the market opportunity and investment opportunities are, and what is the problem you solve and how do you solve it.

Tell the story of your business, but from the point of view of the investor.

A first impression comes in a lot of ways. It's not just did you wear a suit that day, although dressing the part is important.

Does your presentation "dress the part"? If you tell an investor you are a high tech, advanced company and your presentation looks like a word document, there's nothing wrong with that per se, but the impression it leaves may not be everything it needs to be. In this day and age when design, photography and software tools are readily available, it's what you see that leaves an impression. There is no excuse for walking into a presentation and not having it look good for you.

If you don't have the skill set to create a dynamic professional presentation, there are probably people in your network, or an online freelance site that can help you create something that makes a good first impression.

Once you are through the presentation, and we know you will make an awesome presentation, what are the next steps? Follow up. I would venture to say that follow-up is a key habit to success.

It may sound like a lost art, but send a handwritten thank you card. A handwritten thank you card is a very big deal; it shows you appreciated the meeting and the investor's time, by taking your time to personally write the card. While there are companies you can go to online that will write and send out cards for you, it is fine, but it takes away that personal touch.

Assuming the presentation goes well, the investors are going to ask you for information. Be ready to admit what you don't know and promise to get back to them. The key is you may not have all the answers, but with intentional follow up you can get the information to them. There are some questions they will probably ask that you can prepare for, but if they ask you something you don't know, you can tell them you will get the answer and get back to them. Then actually do the follow up. I would strongly suggest that you don't "wing it" when it comes to answering their questions but rather if you don't know the information let them know that you will follow up with that information.

Take notes or have someone there whose only job is to capture and write down all the questions. Investors will give you feedback every time you present. Even if an investor says NO, you'll have a ton of great feedback that you can take into the next meeting. You'll learn as you go and be more prepared for the next presentation. If they all have the same objections or questions, it's a really good place to stop and take a look at your business, and it might be time to pivot or figure out that answer. They are telling you what they are looking for to feel comfortable investing in your deal. Having someone at the meeting that can be the "listening ear" can prove to be very beneficial for you. Often when presenting we are focusing on the point we want to make and may miss some of the vital information. So enlist a team member, colleague or friend to come to the presentation with you.

The ability to write down those questions and then follow up on them, not just to them, but to your internal team too, is very important.

Investors may want to know if your idea or company is 'evolutionary' or 'revolutionary'.

Revolutionary is creating something bigger, better, faster than it is currently. Evolutionary is transforming an industry like Uber, and Airbnb. They completely transform, evolve an industry. Some investors may ask if the investment is recession proof.

A question we typically ask every entrepreneur we meet is 'what problem does your product or service solve?' If we can't get a clear and concise answer that's where we stop as that needs to be addressed right away. If you don't articulate what problem you solve, why are you in business?

And investors want to know if you, the entrepreneur, have the "Right Stuff." It's those characteristics we referred to earlier. The investor is not in your business day-to-day, they aren't the ones making game time decisions, they're not the one hiking the ball, making the pass – that's not their role.

Their role is to work with you, to provide mentorship to you, to provide guidance, to assist you, and provide strategy, but ultimately you are the one with the day-to-day running of the business and they want to feel comfortable that you can produce results.

What percentage of entrepreneurs get investors at each of these levels?

Forty percent of entrepreneurs get their funding from family and friends. That's a good and bad thing. It's good in that it is the one we have most readily available, family and friends. Sometimes, they believe more highly in us and what we can accomplish - more than we do! The good news is their risk aversion is less. They are more likely to want to invest in us.

As you go through the investor types, it becomes more and more about the business than you the entrepreneur. A VC investor would scrutinize us more than our family and friends do. Now they start to underwrite the business to make sure the business has the right stuff.

ABC - Always Be Closing

You always want to be closing. Are you following up and following through? Are you asking for the money? Do you have professionals to assist with the investment? Do you have the right legal documents set up? Are bank accounts set up? Are you complying with State and Federal laws around fundraising and securities? It is so important to make sure you have these things in place.

It could be as simple as you are taking a loan from a sibling, do you have at least a promissory note or the right loan documents? There are lots of solutions out there for anyone's budget that you can get free or low cost documentation. You can get a local attorney to assist you in putting together your deal documentation. The type of investor you are going to will determine the type of documents you will need.

Always consult a professional before selling Securities in your business.

If you are afraid to follow up and ask for that money, you aren't going to get a YES. You need to be willing to do that. If they say NO ask them if they know who the deal might be good for if not for them; ask for a referral. If they DO give you a referral, at least you know they thought you had a good idea, good enough for someone else to consider investing. They wouldn't have given you the referral if they didn't believe the pitch was worth looking at by someone else.

To recap, we looked at finding the right investors and knowing the right investor will determine your game plan moving forward. Be sure you have the right story and the right presentation to make a great first impression. Included in that is what your website looks like, your social media presence, and your presentation to them looks like. All these things are taken into consideration when they go to vet you.

We also reviewed what should be done after the presentation; the follow up and the follow through. When another appointment is set, go to the meeting prepared with the answers to the questions they asked in the initial meeting. When they do agree to fund you, make sure you have the right documents in place to actually close the deal!

Most importantly, remember that they are looking at you to determine if you have the characteristics of successful millionaire and billionaire!

THE VALUE MINDSET

Many people choose to be an entrepreneur based on the lifestyle being entrepreneurial allows, yet as we've discussed, it does not come without hard work, dedication and ultimately the right mindset.

Above all, an entrepreneur's mindset is what will make the difference between success and failure. When we speak of mindset, we are not talking about having a positive attitude based on a social media post or strategies learned in the latest book you have read. We are talking about a shift in behavior and patterns that transforms the way you act and ultimately do business. This entrepreneurial mindset is necessary to create the greatest results for you and your business, which will create success.

Throughout this book we talk about Mindset and Behaviors and how important they are for success. Mindset is based on value – the value that is perceived and realized by the key stakeholders in your life and your business. Your ability to demonstrate value is directly proportional to your ability to create success.

The Value Mindset is understanding that your answer to 'what's in it for me?' has the value that is important to your audience. It is also holding the behaviors and habits that consistently create and reinforce that value within your business.

This value is different for each person you interact with on a daily basis – for your customer, when you demonstrate this Value Mindset they are willing to pay for your product. In fact sometimes they're willing to pay a premium for your product because of perceived value. Value to customers could be flexibility in delivery of your product or service, a venue to express ideas on improvements, quick response time to issues and questions. Making the customer feel that not only your product or service is valuable, but so is your customer. Making them feel you value their business and are willing to go the extra mile to please them, will result on sales, and hopefully return business. On the other hand, without the existence of value, you will not have a customer and you will not have sales. The Sales Funnel and resulting traction (sales) are the top line measurement of the success of the business and rolls down to profitability for the owner.

For your investors or lenders it is necessary to demonstrate value in your business and business model. This value comes from the ability to produce a return, to demonstrate that your projections can be reached based on your leadership, your team and access to mentors, coaches and subject matter experts, The value also comes from your ability to pay back a loan, to grow your business based on a solid strategy. You and your team will need to demonstrate the value you bring to the business as individuals with your ability to produce results in line with the strategy, creating growth and profitability of the business to secure funding. After funding is secured, it is also being a good investment with good communication and updates to your investors, seeking advice and being open to being coached by those more experienced than you or your team. Being open to other viewpoints and showing you are open to learning and expanding will also demonstrate value to your investors.

For the team you surround yourself with, who executes daily on the strategy to reach the vision, they must feel value in the their efforts. This value typically comes from the culture of an organization as well as different forms of compensation. The stronger the culture, the more empowering the organization, the more valuable the team feels and is confident in its willingness to overcome obstacles to create success.

Jacques Panis, President of the Detroit-based company, Shinola, has instilled the high-five culture. He has made it a habit of walking the company and factory floor giving high-fives to the team, of reinforcing how great it is to work at Shinola, and how grateful he is to his team for consistently delivering quality products. You can bet his team feels valued!

Entrepreneurs will often get caught up in how to be successful and what success is - take a moment to think why success is created. Success is created when you can demonstrate value to other people each day.

An entrepreneur's mission should be to create value for the people they interact with, no matter the circumstances. It is this one single element, to demonstrate true value, as to why we have seen great entrepreneurs like Richard Branson, Elon Musk, Steve Jobs and Oprah Winfrey succeed in everything they do.

How do *you* create value? Here are a few questions to get you thinking about the a value-based mindset:

What problem do you solve?

Who do you solve it for?

Why are you the right person/ team to solve it?

Why is now the right time to solve it?

What makes you bigger/ better/ different than your competition?

How do you do what you do faster/ easier/ less expensively?

What do your customers know you for? What would you want to be known for?

How do you create value?

Working with the PRETENDER ENTREPRENEUR

Case Study: *Now you see them, now you don't!*

For years I worked in the media industry and had the opportunity to interact with multiple owners of local and regional companies. I witnessed the Pretender Entrepreneur in action on a weekly basis. This is the Entrepreneur that puts up the front of a successful business, and will do anything not to look bad to anyone. They look to others for validation of who they are instead of looking internally. You'll meet them at industry and networking events and they always proudly tout how successful their venture is going. Their future is always shining bright. But in reality, their business is facing uncertainty. Any growth or start up business will have uncertainty, it is in the risk that growth occurs.

When working with small and medium size businesses, I found that there was a lot of pretending that went on - one day a company was in business, the next, its doors were closed with not even a hint there was a problem. I saw it over and over again. Typically an entrepreneur is trying to look good and avoiding looking bad. Most times I attracted the successful entrepreneurs and those that want to be successful, so I saw my share of pretenders.

When the business started to struggle, they lied, to themselves and to anyone else that there was a problem. They were so busy trying to keep up the façade, and were more concerned about what others would think; they didn't even let their team know they were getting ready to fold the business! They lost out on revenue in their final days because they could not admit to anyone, especially their clients, that they were about to go out of business.

Most of these entrepreneurs didn't really know the business they were in. If they had, they would know that the industry is a difficult one and full of abundant times as well as very lean times. If they had the right business knowledge they could have developed the business strategies to counteract the tough times. Instead they acted as if nothing was wrong, then poof! – they just disappeared from the landscape to reappear working for another business.

If they were not so focused on what others thought, they could have sought out the opinions and guidance of more experienced industry professionals; they could have made deals with advertisers to extend their revenue through the tough times. They could have pushed through and recovered. Because they were fearful of looking bad to others, because they didn't trust in their own abilities, they failed.

I cannot tell you how many times entrepreneurs come to me afterwards as opposed to dealing with the matter in advance or as soon as things start going south.

Lesson: *The Pretender Entrepreneur has little or no regard for their own abilities and looks to the opinions of others for validation. Rather than look weak or inexperienced, they would rather pretend to be successful and fail. If you are, or know a pretender, take the time to get to the bottom of the issues and problems and take the steps to "right the ship" before it is too late.*

THE ENTREPRENEURIAL CULTURE

When we say Entrepreneurial Culture, what does that bring to mind? A pool table in the middle of the workspace, people sitting on bean bags working on laptops? A place where people are video conferencing instead of being physically present for a meeting?

An Entrepreneurial Culture could hold these things and it does sound like fun! And those things help to create a physical culture, not actually a business culture. Culture is the behaviors, values and beliefs of an organization. When you begin to understand those, when you begin to truly create and express yourself and build an ultimate performance state, this is when the culture will truly be expressed. And this is where your culture comes from.

The leaders' and founders' (entrepreneurs') strong beliefs will nourish the team and permeate the business at each level of the organization. Leaders must lead by example; their beliefs, values and behaviors should be modeled by everyone in the organization. Leaders must be very clear of their vision and align the culture accordingly.

One comment we always receive about entrepreneurial culture is that the company is small, it may be one person or a few people or there may not even be an office. Culture, especially an entrepreneurial culture, is not something you wait to create. It is part of your DNA, embedded in the way you make decisions, how you handle processes and systems, what strategy you use to grow your business. Every aspect of the organization is guided by your culture. As we look at organizations, we have found an entrepreneurial culture is about risk taking, continual learning, being receptive to new ideas, encouragement to think beyond the immediate problem with creative solutions and most importantly empowerment of others in your network and on your team. It is about team members who feel they have a say in the running of the company, they are free to move and pivot as they see fit to reach the company's defined outcomes. It an all-encompassing belief that anything can, and will, be accomplished.

The Entrepreneurial Culture can exist in large, corporate environments – it's not limited to startups and small businesses. A company culture reflects what is important to the people leading the business; it is in effect the Identity of a Business.

An Entrepreneurial Culture is an environment that fosters empowerment. There are significant characteristics that are found in most successful Entrepreneurial Cultures and they are reviewed below.

Visionary: The visionary in any culture is all about making a dent in the Universe (like Steve Jobs). The firm and what it produces can be very disruptive to an industry, and have a major impact with a revolutionary product or evolving a current industry and taking it forward in leaps and bounds. This cultural characteristic is both volatile and creative. Success isn't necessarily measured by the numbers, but by the effort and how close to the mark the team came.

Uncertainty: Uncertainty in a culture lives and thrives in the unknown; not knowing if the risks taken will pan out. It is taking that step out and wondering if the abyss is going to swallow them up, or if that bridge they saw spanning the abyss will manifest. This ambiguity can lack certainty and structure. It is unpredictable and the team would need to pivot based on changes that are often times unforeseen. The driving philosophy is based on "What would you do if you could not fail?"

Dynamic: A transformative and impactful – dynamic – culture is one where the energy of everyone is high and excited. The ideas, services and products coming

out of a dynamic culture are game changing. The company is watched by the industry and as they ask 'What are you up to and why?' These are the companies that put other companies out of business and leave them in their dust wondering what happened!

Value: The characteristics above can all coexist, but the Value Characteristic is a very important one. It focuses on the customer, tries to out do the competition by giving more (service, product, etc.) and by doing so, makes a positive difference in a customer's life or business. Often these companies will give away free items (Freemiums) to attract and keep customers. It encourages an emotional connection with the customer at every opportunity. It is all about them and the more the company, its team members and ownership lead with this, the more success they will achieve.

Money: When producing a result, money follows (Sales/Investments). The product or service solves a problem and the sales process is intuitive – you don't need an hour to explain the problem/solution ratio. When you can produce income, you will also produce attention from investors, potential customers and become attractive to prospective employees. Producing sales in and of itself can be an exciting motivator to the team.

Focus: When a company starts to grow, the leadership and team must stay committed and dedicated long after the initial excitement has fallen off. This characteristic is very important because without focus, the long-term goals and outcomes envisioned at the beginning of the venture won't be reached. Focus on the outcomes and setting measurable results is key to success. Throughout this book we emphasize the importance of focus and making sure focus in on the right thing to move a company forward.

Growth: Another characteristic of entrepreneurial cultures is growth. What is the outcome? Build and grow the business or acquisition? Set these growth goals and constantly nurture the team to achieve the goals. The Growth focused entrepreneurial culture will have a 1-year, 3-year and 5-year plan. One of the basic human emotional needs is growth and as an entrepreneurial culture, it is important to feed this need. There is a great quote in the movie Shawshank Redemption where the lead character says "Get busy living, or get busy dying." What are you and your organization going to do today, this week, this month, this year to grow?

Investment: We hear the word "investment" and think of someone putting money into our business. In the cultural sense, it's a willingness by the leaders and team to invest their time, money, and energy in the short-term for long-term gain. The investment can be to clients (invest in technology you can use to service them), vendors (getting deep discounts as you start out) and team members (through education, flexible hours, challenging responsibilities). When properly done investing in a team will produce a return. One of the keys here is making investments in your company with the same level of sophistication and due diligence that a savvy businessperson makes for their financial investments.

Relationship: An entrepreneur typically does not work and grow a business in isolation, it is with a team or community that an idea is nurtured and grows. By relating in a real and authentic manner, a community can be built of supporters, believers, and future customers. Having strong relationships can triple the bottom line. Ultimately, the ability to build strong relationships with others, both internal and external, can lead to abundance in many regards.

All these characteristics are usually found at some level in most companies that foster a healthy entrepreneurial culture. As a company grows, it will become more difficult to maintain an entrepreneurial culture. Therefore, as it begins to hire a team, bring on board only those that demonstrate some or all of these characteristics. If you want an entrepreneurial environment, hire entrepreneurial people! Hiring a team that understands the outcome is a shared and collaborative effort to reach is important. Therefore it is very important, as early as possible, to plan the seeds for your culture, to start out on the right foot; to build it from the beginning.

Building an entrepreneurial team that achieves results, and cultivating an entrepreneurial culture will result in success!

THE 4 AREAS SUCCESSFUL ENTREPRENEURS EXCEL IN

What does it mean to have the Identity of an Entrepreneur we talk about?

What we're talking about in this identity is the possession of certain characteristics that an individual who considers himself an entrepreneur exhibit that make up who they are and how they do business.

What's been really awesome in my experiences is that I've learned and been mentored in these characteristics. Now, in this part of my career, I've begun to coach and work with various entrepreneurs through the process of attending pitch competitions, Angel investing, through fundraising efforts, and legal work.

From my own experience working with hundred of entrepreneurs, I've been able to identify and better understand and identify where real success comes from.

What we've found is that these successful entrepreneurs excel in 4 key areas: Business Knowledge, Business Strategy, Business Development, Mindset and Behaviors.

The first area is Business Knowledge. Business Knowledge is that understanding of your industry and knowing your competitors. It's taking the time to dig deep to really do the research. We've all done research papers at some point in our educations. They are not always the most fun, but when you are done, you wrote the paper and you could speak about it, you knew it and you understood it. In certain situations you found solutions to problems.

Getting started on securing your Business Knowledge could be a simple as going online, finding a role model and see what books on business they are reading. Then read those books. This type of reading is all about gaining knowledge. Then expand your research into what your competition is doing, how they are marketing, what new trends are in the industry you are in and figuring out how to adapt to those trends and changes. Read business books, marketing books, how to hire for your culture, read articles and posts on subjects to your business and industry. The outcome you will be focused on is to be fully knowledgeable on your industry, and how to run your business. Just like when you wrote the research papers, you want to be the expert for your business.

As an Entrepreneur you are constantly looking for ways to be more resourceful, to be able to deal with uncertainty, to be more creative, to be able to take new risks, to be able to come up with new business models, to be able to address your team, to be a better leader, to create success in your personal and professional life. You're looking for all those things. Assuming your mindset is there, it comes down to, do you have the knowledge, do you understand, do you know your industry inside and out?

There's a saying, a great book, [Outliers, by Malcolm Gladwell: *http://gladwell. com/outliers/the-10000-hour-rule/*] that states that it takes 10,000 hours to become a guru. Are you on your way to being a guru?

When you look at most successful people that have the identity of success in whatever their profession happens to be, it didn't happen overnight. They gained a knowledge base; they understood they were a student. In sports we say they were a student of the game. To say it a different way, some of the greatest musicians, played hundreds of thousands of performances before they ever made their actual debut.

I'm a published author four times over. I look back on the many hours of research, of knowledge, of studying that went into being prepared to write each book, and how many times they were edited and revised to get to a final printed copy. I definitely understand the amount of knowledge that it took to get there; being successful in business is the exact same thing.

As an entrepreneur you also need to have a certain amount of knowledge, and the quicker you can surround yourself with people, with other individuals who can provide what you may lack, the better off you'll be. That is why advisors and mentors are so important; they can be great resources to help give you knowledge, to build that 'tribal' knowledge. Finding the right professionals, accountants, lawyers, insurance agents, and other professionals to surround yourself with that can provide your 'tribal' knowledge can be so helpful.

In building a Board of Directors, while it looks good and it does build credibility, but it's the *knowledge base* that is so important. These are people you will be able to turn to because they are industry experts or subject matter experts and they will give you knowledge is invaluable.

When you think about having a strategic partner or strategic investor, that is about trying to find someone with that knowledge base that willingly brings that knowledge and strategy to the table. Business Knowledge is the first area for you to excel in for you to find success in your business.

When you speak to people in Real Estate, good agents know their industry inside and out, the same with Film Producers, they know how the whole movie process works, inside and out. When you talk to a great lawyer, they know the law inside and out. They've all built that knowledge base.

When you talk to a great botanist, they know how to grow a plant or run a florist inside and out. One entrepreneur I'm very intrigued with owns a super hyper local sustainable teashop in my town, and he's a botanist! He understands how the plants grow. Do you think he knows how to make great tea and coffee? Absolutely! He studied and has the knowledge and applied the knowledge in an unexpected way!

Let's move on to another area of focus, Business Strategy. How can you begin to put together a playbook when you don't know where you are going or don't have any idea how to get there? This is why so often, to use a sports analogy, teams spend so much time between games, professional pitchers spend so much time between starts, defensive and offensive coordinators spend time studying, gaining the knowledge so that when it's time to put the playbook together, to build that strategy, they the have a background of knowledge to build from.

In Business Strategy, it's really your plan of action, that's what you're going to look to execute on. You don't just haphazardly 'fire, ready, aim.' You aim, then you get ready, then you fire. You follow the right steps to be successful. When you have the right strategy, you have a chance to know where you area able to go, take steps, create accountability and execute. You are able to put those puzzle pieces together to connect to get the results you are ultimately looking for.

Once you have the strategy, you can start to build out the operations of the business. What does your business look like in a year from now? Figure that out and then build back the strategy it takes to get there. You're building out a financial model. If you know your goal is X in a year, what do you need to do today to increase it tomorrow, to increase it again to ultimately reach that goal? If your goal is to hit X number of dollars, say five million dollars, in a week, in a quarter, in a year, and that's your goal, you have to have a plan to get there; that's where strategy comes in.

If you don't have the right resources to meet that target goal, you're just shooting darts into the air and there's no target. There's no dartboard, no strategy. It's important to have that strategy. Even Tic Tac Toe requires knowledge and strategy behind the moves to win each time.

When you are doing any sport, when you are doing business, when you are doing life, strategy comes into play. Once you have the right beliefs and the capabilities in place you can execute on a strategy to get those results. We take a great deal of time to ensure entrepreneurs have the right beliefs, the right mindset and from there, they are able to get the right capabilities to surround themselves with, and once they have those two pieces, they can execute on their Strategy.

Strategy is so important because it encompasses everything on how you are going to handle your business (the HR component, the culture, etc.) all those things become very important if not critical when you start to develop your strategy and how to execute it.

The next area we move into after that is Business Development. Let's assume you have all the right pieces in place and the business is working. You've put it all together. You've used your research to develop your Business Strategy.

Your business is moving along; you can deliver your product or services. You've actually defined that there is a problem that you solve with your product or services, and you can now deliver that solution. What comes next? Business Development.

Business Development is a lot of things and we're going to take a few minutes to talk about each one of them. When you think of Business Development, you think of sales. It is having a plan for sales and being able to go out and get those sales. Do you know who your customer is? Do you know how to speak to that customer? How to present to that customer? How to close that customer deal? Do you know the pricing around that customer? What does your sales funnel look like? How are you managing your sales? All that stuff is included in the right Business Strategy, and then executing on the Business Development side. So for sales, you have to have that strategy to execute on the Business Development.

Next, look at Marketing. You should include a section about Marketing in your Strategy. When you move to Business Development it is executing, having a Marketing Plan and executing on it that produces results that have a return on your investment (ROI). Public Relations (PR) can also fit into your Marketing plan.

When we discuss the Internet there's a whole other world we're talking about. We're talking about Social Media, digital marketing, content marketing; all those things are part of you doing the research to then build the strategy, to then focus on that Business Development and execution component.
In some startups we call it 'growth Hacking' that ability to figure out how to develop business using the Internet, direct response, email and Social Media. The execution of your Marketing Plan is the Business Development component of the four areas.

At the end of the day, if you are a start up business, sales are really important. It shows proof of concept, it attracts investors and it brings revenue in to overcome obstacles and hire team members. Startups cannot afford to ignore Business Development if they wish to grow.

If you are in a growth stage company, sales are important as well. If you get some funding or are looking to attract money, showing growth is a great a way to get it. There is nothing better than to walk into an investor meeting and being able to say "last quarter we were up X percent." It is important from a Business Development standpoint to assist in continuing to grow.

For successful companies that have gone public, what will you do now to meet shareholder profitability? It's still about Business Development. You may just have a successful company, and you're looking for a succession plan or to exit, at that point, how do you continue to do Business Development? Maybe it's a cash cow business and you don't want to get rid of it, and as Entrepreneurs that's a great place to be, so how do you then take the time to be able to make sure you can continue that Business Development, that it doesn't fall off, lose the energy? No matter what business stage your company is at; Business Development is key to moving it forward to the next stage of development.

That's all part of driving the revenue, of growing the business. Do you have a culture that allows you to do that? Taking the Business Knowledge to develop Business Strategy, the plan, and then to execute the plan is Business Development. It includes sales, marketing, internal operations of a business including growth and exit strategies.

The last area successful entrepreneurs excel in is Mindset and Behavior. While we discuss it last, it is the most important because it is the basis and foundation for everything.

If you ask successful Entrepreneurs what is the most important thing they can attribute their success to, they may not use the words mindset and behavior, but they talk about discipline, being focused, overcoming obstacles or challenges and being able to deal with doubt or uncertainty. They speak about how to be empowering, how to be visionary.

That's what we're talking about with Mindset and Behavior. As we mentioned in an earlier chapter, a recent study published by oDesk stated 90 percent of people believe that entrepreneurialism is a mindset. Being an Entrepreneur starts with your mindset. If you don't have the right mindset then you're not going to make it through the Business Knowledge step, you're not going to take the time to get the Business Strategy in place, you're not going to be focused or outcome oriented to the business culture at hand.

If you don't have the right mindset, even if you do make it through Business Knowledge and Business Strategy, you're going to hit Deception and have to overcome obstacles when it gets to Business Development. The right mindset can drive you through all three of the other areas.

When we look at successful people like Warren Buffet or Bill Gates, when they talk about being an entrepreneur, they talk about how interpersonal development is so important to their success. When you look at successful leaders and business owners, and you go back and look a what they've done, they focused on growing themselves as an individual and they focused on growing their organizations from a culture standpoint.

There was always an assumption that their product or service solved a problem, that it had a demand in the marketplace, and then they were able to focus on what really created that growth, what really created that success. It was all about the mindset and the behavior.

Business Knowledge, **Business Strategy**, **Business Development** and **Mindset** and **Behavior**, were the areas we found repeatedly that successful entrepreneurs excel in. They and their organizations know how to create a lasting impact in these four areas to create growth in their organizations, transform and overcome obstacles, to ultimately create successful identities in their organization.

To be successful, you, and/or your team, need to excel in these areas too!

Working with the STRESSED ACHIEVER ENTREPRENEUR

Case Study: *I'm almost there!*

The Entrepreneur who is a Stressed Achiever is very, very driven, and often times very successful – but at a cost.

While there is a distinct difference between Delegation and Abdication in working with a team, the Stressed Achiever Entrepreneur only thinks he delegates. He is the manager that must be included on all emails, and while he may have assigned responsibility to others, he's still very hands on and involved in all projects. He's the one that asks for the status well before the deadline, never giving the team the pleasure of handing over a finished deliverable, on time, effectively making the team feel incompetent. This entrepreneur works 'in' the business, instead of 'on' the business.

This is the entrepreneur who insists more people attend a meeting than necessary. His stress ultimately permeates his organization and stresses everyone around him. He is results driven – at any cost. He is almost aggressive in his approach grinding to produce results. He pulls everyone along with him, whether they can keep up and meet his expectations it or not.

The "Holy Grail" mentality is very prevalent with the Stressed Achiever – if they can just get what they want, they'll be happy. But once that goal is attained, they immediately have a new goal to focus on.

And the Stressed Achiever Entrepreneur will reach his goals, all of them. However, in pushing through the obstacles, through Deception, he'll push through like a linebacker, and never take the time to work and grow in the process. The casualties pile up along the way. He'll lose not just team members, but will kill morale and the company culture.

I've worked with multiple Stressed Achievers at the helm of a successful companies. They demonstrated all of these characteristics. In fact, one in particular always wanted results, and he got them, but along the way there were a lot of casualties. Good people with confidence in their abilities finally left his organization, beaten down and, demoralized.

It was amazing to watch this leader finally realize that the joy is in the journey not the destination. He realized the happiness he sought wasn't in the goals he set, but how he attained them. The old saying 'it trickles from the top down' is very true; as this leader relaxed, stepped back a let his team handle their assignments, they became more confident, less stressed and the morale went up noticeably, and staff resignations were greatly reduced.

When the Stressed Achiever realizes the pain they've caused around them and they wake up, often it's too late.

Lesson: Do not seek happiness for the achievements, but in the journey toward your achievements. Remember that as the leader, your energy will permeate your entire organization.

SUCCESS

Success. That word has as many facets as any diamond, and can be just as brilliant and definitely more valuable. Ultimately, everyone loves success and achieving really depends on one's personal perspective.

How does one measure success?

That's an interesting question, because for each person, there is a different measurement. In business success can be measured by the company's profitability, or securing funding for its growth beyond the initial start up phase, or creating a 'Unicorn' company (companies that have soared to a $1 billion valuation or higher, based on fundraising). As well, it could be a well-executed launch of a product; it could be watching, coaching and mentoring staff to stretch beyond what they thought they could achieve; it could be attracting the right investors to grow to the next level and it could be a successful exit strategy.

For some, success is measured on a more personal level rather than financial level. Being a successful spouse, parent, son or daughter, friend or sibling can be seen as success, especially if working a demanding job or being the entrepreneur leader of a start up.

Success can be an ending, attaining a goal, the completion of a journey. Or success can be the beginning of the journey, finally taking that first step with confidence and excitement. Having the ability to give back, pay for a child's college, or have the personal freedom to travel and play how we see fit are also measures of success.

Entrepreneurs, small business owners and independent contractors or freelancers are looking for collaboration, growth and success. Often to these groups, success is working when they want, where they want on what they want. Remember, 90% of people think that entrepreneurship is a mindset. Not owning a business, but rather a mindset.

When we look to some of the great leaders and entrepreneurs of our generation, they talk about that it is important to fail, because on the other side of failure is success. These individuals like Steve Jobs, Richard Branson, Marcus Lemonis and Elon Musk talk about the growth mindset and the fact that the mind can be strengthened like a muscle. They talk about how individuals willing to take a risk can change the world. They talk about how mindset helps individuals create better solutions in their businesses. And they talk about how people can reinvent and fix any business situation. They talk about the same things we shared with you in this book.

One way to think about it is that most entrepreneurs want to achieve success for their business and want their growth to look like this:

In actuality, it looks more like this:

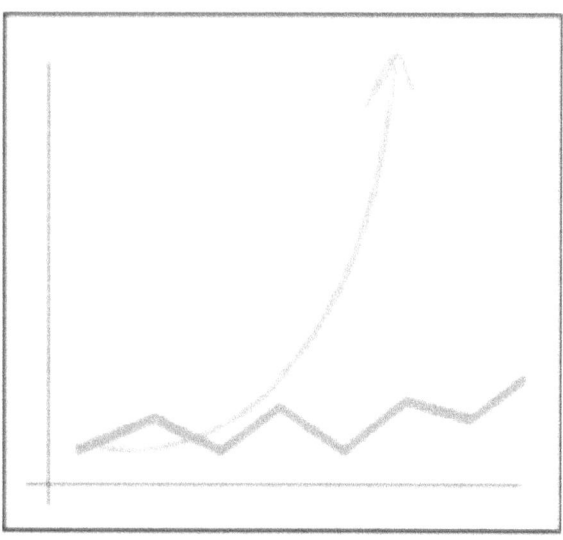

How to you create growth?

The answer lies in your ability to be successful; you as an individual, you as a team to be successful.

Success is always defined by each individual, and success is still being driven by outcomes, success is staying focused, success is being internally motivated, success is having the ideal beliefs, success is dealing with uncertainty – no matter if your definition is personal or for your business.

For business, entrepreneurs start very excited and they think they just have to take one step or do one thing, or complete one task and they're going to have success; it's actually not one step or one task, and as we've repeatedly said, it's a journey. And quite often the journey takes a while and has some points where you fall down and have to get back up to ultimately get to the other side (Cycle of Growth).

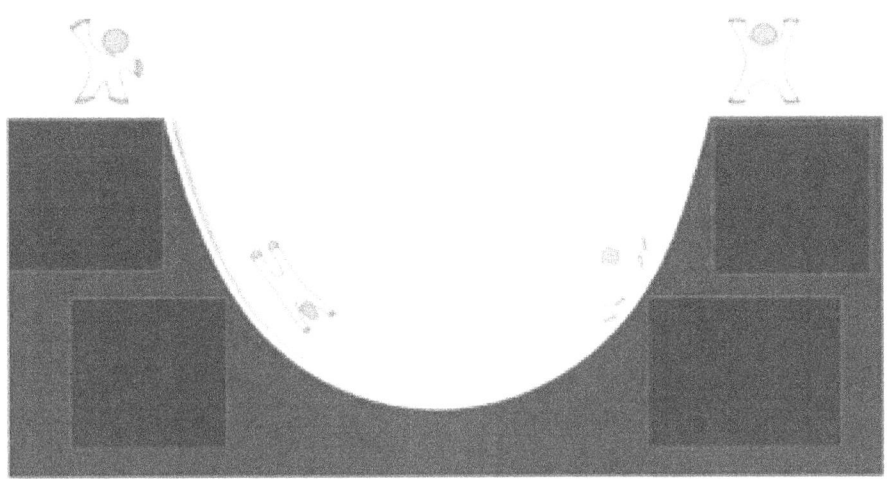

And quite honestly, it's not just one experience like this; it's a series of experiences like this that over time lead to growth. The growth that looks a lot like that success curve we talked about above.

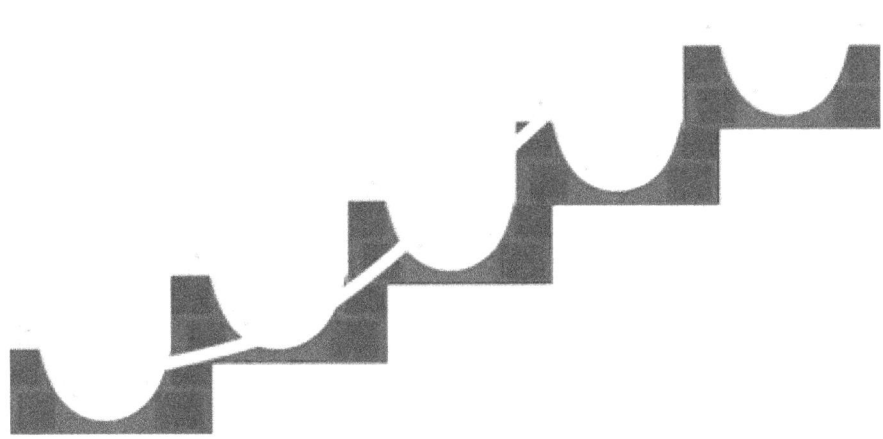

Everyone has his or her own measuring stick. We are not dictating to you what *your* measurement of success should be; rather we are giving you the tools you need to reach the identity of a successful person, both professionally and personally. These skills can be used to reach a balance in your life and help you create abundance physically, mentally, emotionally, and spiritually.

These tools will help you have a successful life. Knowing what success means to you is the first step in creating a vision of your future.

Working with the SUCCESS SEEKER ENTREPRENEUR

Case Study: *Relax, you made it!*

We're all seeking some form of success as an entrepreneur, right? Of course. Part of being in business is the success - great team, nice office, amazing customers, financial abundance and work life balance. The Success Seeker Entrepreneur I'm referring to is wants these things too – only she's already there!

I worked with an entrepreneur who received a great deal of accolades, awards and media exposure from local publications as well as nominations to national awards. She was a positive person, always looked at life as a glass half full. She was always seeking to grow and better herself.

She did Yoga, ran marathons, meditated, did Tai Chi, went to personal and professional growth classes and focused on growth spiritually and physically, as well as in business.

What's interesting is that she was always seeking success and didn't feel like a success. We saw her and valued her as a successful, well-balanced person, but that's not how she saw herself.

Every time Deception crept up on her she looked to others for confidence and validation. She looked outside herself, not stopping to appreciate the path she was on, the ups and downs, the bumps in the road - the things that make the journey interesting. She didn't gain happiness from the journey and uncertainty; she was hell bent on getting to a place of certainty. A place that is elusive and ever changing for entrepreneurs.

When she faced actually doing Business Development, she floundered, looking to experts to push her product and had them become the spokesperson, when she knew the product, the pros, the cons, and how to offset any argument and turn a 'no' into a 'yes'. She found a solution, but not the most ideal; she would have been the better choice, but not having the confidence, she relied on others who did.

When she went to develop her marketing, she had really creative and different ideas on how to promote the product, but let them be pushed to the side by 'experts' that didn't have her business knowledge. They didn't know her industry, her customer, or her product as well as she did. While the campaigns garnered notice and sales increased, if she had followed her intuition, the results could have been so much more. Once sales were there, she drove herself forward without so much as a break in stride, instead of sitting back for a bit and enjoying the moment.

She was always looking to that next goal to reach, the next level of success.

She didn't realize she was already there!

Lesson: You already have what you need to be a success; just look inside yourself. Judging your success through third parties, awards and media exposure are false measurements of a life.

BE
INVESTABLE

What is Success?

SUCCESS IS...

being driven by Outcomes

SUCCESS IS...

staying Focused

SUCCESS IS...

staying Focused

SUCCESS IS...

being Internally Motivated

SUCCESS IS...

having the Ideal Beliefs

SUCCESS IS...

dealing with Uncertainty

NEXT STEPS

Sign Up For:

- A **FREE** Copy of THE SIMPLE SECRETS OF FUNDRAISING
- A **FREE** Course – The Art Of Fundraising, available Exclusively on Udemy.com
- A **FREE** Event to attend either in person of via webinar

Participate In:

- Our Daily Success Program and get Daily Success Tasks sent to your inbox
- Our Summaries 2 Success Program and get weekly book reviews

Enroll In:

- The Investable Concept Series
- The Investable Blueprint
- One of our Other Amazing Programs

STEP

1

SIGN UP FOR...

Your FREE copy of our eBook, the SIMPLE SECRETS OF FUNDRAISING.

The biggest problem entrepreneurs and small businesses face today is funding for their idea, invention or business. Is securing funding really that difficult or a mystic quest full of myths as to the conquest? We believe it is not any more difficult than making a sale for their business.

We don't think fundraising is impossible, rather an obstacle, a challenge that requires the right focus, beliefs, capabilities and strategies to achieve. Our eBook goes over the myths, the obstacles, and what exactly it means to demonstrate their ability to Be Investable.

If you are looking to build an investable company, download your copy today!

Download Link: http://www.getinvestable.com/ssofr

SIGN UP FOR...

Learn what venture Capitalists and Investors look for in Investable Companies with this free course through UDEMY! Attendees will learn how to build investable companies and become an investable entrepreneur. Changing a mindset to one that thinks about a business opportunity in terms of investability from the investor's point of view and taking the risk out of a business opportunity are just a few of the things taught in the course.

If you want to understand what investors are looking for when determining what businesses to support with funding, you won't want to miss this free course!

Course Link: https://www.udemy.com/the-art-of-raising-capital/

STEP 1

SIGN UP FOR...

One of the easiest ways to learn about anything is through an event. We hold events throughout the country and monthly webinars on the topics that are important to all entrepreneurs – no matter the product, sector or target market, no matter the development stage of the business.

These free events are answer so many of the questions entrepreneurs and small business owners ask about fundraising – how to know when they are ready to seek outside investment, how to determine the best investors to contact, what key characteristics to demonstrate, what type of entrepreneur they are and how likely are they to secure funding. We even discuss the properties that should be outlined in The Pitch Deck!

Sign up today on our site for our next event. These events have proven to be key to the success of many entrepreneurs – we know they can help you succeed too!

Link: http://www.getinvestable.com/events

PARTICIPATE IN...

One simple task delivered to your email inbox that will help you focus on what's important to you and your business. This Daily Success program provides tasks that are simple and relevant to your everyday life. Daily wins help propel participants forward, keep them on track to reach their goals, and help them to work on the business, not in the business. Daily focus is on key business and fundraising areas that will promote growth, stability and leadership.

This daily program will motivate and keep participants accountable. This is a daily, easy and simple commitment to you and your business. The tasks are geared toward the leader that wants to grow their business, create a culture that can grow with the business, and wants to hire and empower team members.

A simple task that can be done anywhere, anytime to help you focus on your business and its growth! Sign up to participate today!

Link: http://www.getinvestable.com/programs

STEP 2

PARTICIPATE IN...

Our Complimentary Summaries 2 Success Program &
Get Weekly Book Reviews

Have you ever read 4 books in 1 day?

Now you can! Sign up today for instant access to 4 of our bestselling book summaries designed for you to squeeze CENTURIES of knowledge into just MINUTES.

Our team has scoured the universe looking for those books that have made a meaningful impact on readers to Be Investable. After speaking with some of the top experts and conduct research over the last decade, we finally assembled the list of 52 books you must read. BUT, we realize that you are not going to have the time to read, so why not sign up and get a summary each week delivered directly to your inbox.

Gain the insight and wisdom from amazing authors like Napolean Hill, Peter Drucker, Sir Richard Branson and Malcom Gladwell.

Link: http://www.getinvestable.com/programs

ENROLL IN...

Obtain the funding you need to succeed.

With the Be Investable program, you finally have a roadmap for hacking fundraising, attracting mentors and manifesting investors based on your ultimate potential as the leader the ecosystem needs you to be. But what makes this unique is the **TOOL and METHOD by which you learn to do this**.

Link: http://www.getinvestable.com/programs

STEP 3

ENROLL IN...

The Be Investable Series

Be Investable Series is designed for people looking for a fundraising training program that goes into subject matter around become investable and creating an investable business.

The biggest problem entrepreneurs and small businesses face today is funding for their idea, invention or business.

Based on many obsolete models for fundraising and many people's relationship to money and wealth, people stay stuck in states of fear, embarrassment, guilt and confusion and a belief that fundraising is impossible.

Each entrepreneur and business owner has the possibility of securing funding for their idea, invention or business far beyond their current beliefs.

Link: http://www.getinvestable.com/programs

BeInvestable

ENROLL IN...

Entrepreneur Blueprint is our most popular course and has been utilized by some of the most successful entrepreneurs and business minds to obtain the funding necessary to build companies creating massive impact and global change.

Be Investable Is Designed For People Looking For An Advanced Fundraising Training Program - Not For Beginners Or Intermediates, As This Program Goes into Subject Matter that Many Consider Confidential or Unattainable.

Investable

STEP **3**

ENROLL IN...

One Of Our Other Amazing Programs

Entrepreneur Training

Entrepreneur Training course takes you to the next level. Over a 30-day period, you will not only learn the secrets of being a successful entrepreneur, but internalize them into your own belief system, so that it becomes a natural extension of your skill set and entrepreneurial personality. You'll become accustomed to the entrepreneurial habit and mindset necessary to be successful. And you'll be equipped with the tools you need to consistently break through.

4 Colors of Influence

Do you find that some conversations feel easy and enjoyable while others feel like a boxing match? Do you notice you connect instantly with some people yet others you want to throw your hands up and wish the conversation would simply end?

The 4 Colors of Entrepreneurial Influence will accelerate your entrepreneurial success, highlight your business acumen and help you align with and influence anyone!

Be Investable

This program is built around creating consistent habits and staying focused on your entrepreneurial vision. We'll explore what it means to be internally motivated and lead yourself before effectively leading and influencing others around you and your business.

OR, if you are not ready to enroll in one of our programs, head back to Steps 1 & 2 to sign up and participate in our content and courses.

In THE SIMPLE SECRETS OF BEING AN ENTREPRENEUR, Michael S. Melfi shares all the knowledge and wisdom gained from billionaire mentors and millionaire clients.

Michael has been fortunate enough to work with many successful (and not so successful - remember 90% of businesses are out of business in 5 years) entrepreneurs and business people over the years. In these experiences, he gained an inside look into what it takes to not only make it in business but thrive!

The book covers:
- Uncovering the secret characteristics that successful entrepreneurs all have in common?
- How to create focus to have the characteristics of successful entrepreneurs.
- Your Entrepreneurial Type (did you know there was such a thing?)
- Tips and tricks of creating an entrepreneurial culture

Purchase on Amazon.com: http://amzn.com/1530885752

is the ultimate playbook for using Social Media in business. In the book written by Michael Melfi, you will get a play by play on how to utilize Social Media strategies for your company. It is essentially a breakdown of how to execute a digital solution for your online problems and needs. The digital solution provides various marketing and promotional initiatives, very similar to a traditional marketing campaign. Over the pages of this book, the reader will achieve some amazing results utilizing various Social Media platforms and digital strategies. By the end of this book the reader will be able to achieve three goals: COMMUNITY DEVELOPMENT, TRUSTED & AUTHENTIC COMMUNICATION, and ACTION.

Purchase on Amazon.com: http://amzn.to/1TABK2G

Crowdfunding is changing the way we do business. An opportunity is arising for small and big business people to participate in a multi-billion dollar emerging market. This book is for people who are curious about the industry, or for people who know it, love it, and want to learn more. The book will cover where the industry came from, current trends, and how to be successful during and after a crowdfunding campaign. When it comes to the success of a campaign, one must go back to the basics - marketing is creating a clear and concise message to a target demographic, and the result is an increase in funding for that project. Utilize these strategies outline in this book to create a plan to execute for yourself. With this book you will learn to develop a target funding audience, how to ask for money, and get it. This will ultimately assist you in realizing your business vision.

Purchase on Amazon.com: http://amzn.to/24pBrN8

This book is designed to provide information and motivation to our readers. This book is presented solely for educational and entertainment purposes. The author and publisher are not offering it as legal, accounting, or other professional services advice, and as such should not be used as a substitute for consultation with professional accounting, tax, legal or other competent advisors. No warranties or guarantees are expressed or implied by the author's choice to include any of the content in this book. The individual author shall not be liable for any physical, psychological, emotional, financial, or commercial damages, including, but not limited to, special, incidental, consequential or other damages. Every company is different and the advice and strategies contained herein may not be suitable for your situation. You should seek the services of a competent professional before beginning any (business improvement) program. Our views and rights are the same: You are responsible for your own choices, actions, and results.